TREES OF THE CELTIC SAINTS:
the ancient yews of Wales

Trees of the Celtic Saints:

the ancient yews of Wales

Andrew Morton

Published with the financial support
of the Welsh Books Council

ISBN: 978-1-84527-173-2

Cover design: Sian Parri

First published in 2009 by
Gwasg Carreg Gwalch
12 Iard yr Orsaf, Llanrwst, Wales LL26 0EH
tel: 01492 624031
fax: 01492 641502
email: books@carreg-gwalch.com
internet: www.carreg-gwalch.com

To Maureen
and in memory of Robert

Acknowledgements

Particularly:

Staff at the Welsh Archaeological Trusts of Cambria, Glamorgan-Gwent, Gwynedd and
CPAT, Welshpool for their help
and for allowing access to documents and records in their care.

Lecturing and Library staff at University of Wales, Lampeter.

National Library of Wales, Aberystwyth.

The Ancient Yew Group.

Staff at Gwasg Carreg Gwalch.

Robert Bevan-Jones, Stephen Dennis and the late Donald Gregory.

Contents

Foreword

Canon Patrick Thomas

My first incumbency was as Rector of Llangeitho in Ceredigion, the church made famous by the great eighteenth-century preacher Daniel Rowland, who is buried below the chancel step. Between the gate and the church porch were four enormous yew trees. Two (at least) were hollow. One had a door attached to it, so that the gravedigger could keep his implements safely inside. The other had been used in an earlier era to store the coal that had provided heat for the church at that time.

Caron, the village shopkeeper, who was also my churchwarden, had a countryman's unromantic view of the yews. "*Hen goed brwnt ydyn nhw*" ("They're messy old trees"), he once remarked. For me, however, they had a profound fascination, particularly when I heard that they were said to be over a thousand years old.

Those Llangeitho yews had witnessed key events in Welsh cultural and religious history. Rhydderch ap Ieuan Llwyd, the fourteenth-century patron of poets to whom we are indebted for the text of the *Mabinogion* in *Llyfr Gwyn Rhydderch*, would have passed them on his way to hear the *offeren* in St Ceitho's church. The monks of Ystrad Fflur would have ridden by them as they went to visit the convent of Llanllŷr. The trees would also have witnessed the Llangeitho Revival of the 1760s, when Daniel Rowland's ecstatic followers jumped for joy in the churchyard, to the horror of the local archdeacon.

Andrew Morton's superb study not only inspires thoughts of the Llangeitho yew trees, but also suggests to me that my fascination with them may have had its source in a much deeper memory. I spent my early childhood in Buttington in Montgomeryshire, and I learn from this book that there is a yew tree in the churchyard there that is reputed to be 1200 years old. No doubt many other readers will find equally fascinating information about yew trees in places that form a part of their family history.

This volume will take its place alongside the late Major Francis Jones's work on the holy wells of Wales as an invaluable resource for anyone seeking to examine the spiritual topography of our country. Its author is to be congratulated for such a pioneering piece of research presented in an accessible and informative manner.

Patrick Thomas
Carmarthen

Introduction

'Wales probably has the largest collection of ancient yews in the world'
Robert Bevan-Jones, 2002

The common yew (*Taxus baccata*) has long been associated with the churchyards of Britain and Ireland. Although in Ireland the oldest specimens are now gone, in England, Scotland and Wales some veterans can still be found today. Of these countries Wales has the highest concentration of old yews, with over forty trees that can be classified as 'ancient'.

Arriving at a simple description of an 'ancient' yew is not straightforward, as not only are the trees difficult to measure due to the uneven and often split trunks, they can also be much rotted and broken. For this publication the criteria used for 'ancient' is a yew measuring over or near 8 metres in girth and showing various characteristics of great age. The height of the tree is irrelevant for estimating age. In fact ancient yews often have low squat crowns. The main bole (trunk) gives us the biggest clue. It should show hollowing and have advanced decay with bits of decaying heartwood accumulating in the hollow centre. Sometimes only the outer bark remains as a shell and pieces of remaining dead wood bleach over the passing centuries. Internal and secondary stems are usually but not always evident. On occasions these may almost fill the hollow centre of the tree.

The tree should be measured at the narrowest point below 1.5 metres above the surrounding ground level (measured at the highest point of the surrounding ground).

Almost without exception the trees listed within this book grow in churchyards. The association of churchyard and yew is relatively poorly documented, with previous publications concentrating on either the churchyard or the yew and not researching the two subjects together to see if there are links that could shed light on both histories.

The yews of Britain are traditionally regarded as amongst the oldest living plants in Europe. The oldest are to be found mainly in the south-east and south-west of England, excluding Cornwall, and as already mentioned, Wales and her borders.

A notable exception is the yew growing in Fortingall churchyard, Glen Lyon, Perthshire. This tree is regarded by many as the oldest tree in Europe. The fact that it grows in a churchyard within a glen that is closely associated with the Irish abbot and scholar St Adomnan, combined with the fact that elsewhere in Scotland ancient yews are a rarity, leads one to wonder if there is a connection between the oldest surviving yew trees and the activities of the early Celtic saints.

Another paradox concerns the ancient yews of Ireland. From old literature sources and a relatively reliable record from the twelfth century, mention is made of yews growing on ecclesiastical sites in Ireland. It is now no longer possible to find any truly ancient yews in Ireland, and there is no record of their demise after the twelfth century.

In recent years interest has been shown in trying to determine the age of the old yews. Whereas some people seem to have underestimated their ages at around 600 years old, another body of opinion has made claims of some yews being anywhere between 3,000 to 9,000 years old. These assessments are based on either pure speculation or bits of botanical and dendrochronological evidence (see section 'Measuring and ageing yews', p. 18), and show little regard for any archaeological, historical or cultural aspects from the sites on which the trees grow. By viewing the subject from a wider perspective, and bringing together the strands of archaeology, botany and literature, more light may be shed on the association of churchyard and yew, and a more accurate age range put forward for the oldest yews.

In this book particular emphasis is given to several potentially rewarding sites that have ancient yews, and have also received a higher degree of historical and archaeological attention than most of the other Welsh churchyards. Selected from the locations that hold 8-metre-girthed yews are Defynnog in Breconshire, Gwytherin and Llangernyw in Conwy, and Llanerfyl and Pennant Melangell in Montgomeryshire. It is thought that by studying a limited number of sites in greater depth, greater knowledge of the subject as a whole may accrue. A definitive answer to age and association may not exist, but it is hoped this book will increase the available knowledge to those who wish to delve further into this fascinating subject.

Included in this book is a list of 100 of the best yew tree sites in Wales. This 'travelogue' has been arranged region by region. Not all of the trees written about come into the truly 'ancient' category, but all are deemed worthy of note, either because they display ancient characteristics or grow in historic places etc. All these places are churchyard sites or have ecclesiastical connections, so visits take one on a tour of the rich history of Wales from the early medieval period onwards.

Good exploring!

Chapter One

Previous Literature on the Yew

The first major study on the yew in Britain was carried out by the physician John Lowe in the late nineteenth century. In the preface to his work *The Yew Trees of Great Britain and Ireland* of 1897 he commented that some years earlier he had commenced an inquiry into the 'peculiarities' in the rate of growth of yew trees. Included in his records are seven Welsh yews from six locations: Pantllydw, Betws-Newydd, Llanthewy Fach (*Llanddewi Fach*) – a tree lost since 1897 – Mamheilad, Llanfoist and two trees at Goytre.

Lowe's interests included the entomology of the yews, their geographical distribution and estimated ages. For the latter he reviewed de Candolle's calculation methods and exhaustively considered the effect that the 'welding' of young shoots could have on growth rings. He also noted the growth of internal stems within some hollow yew trunks. John Lowe considered why yews were planted in churchyards and concluded his work with historical notes on some of the more well known trees, including the yews at the Welsh churchyards of Gresford (*Gresffordd*), Guilsfield (*Cedigfa*), Mamheilad, and the now 'lost' yew at Llanthewy Fach (*Llanddewi Fach*). Lowe can be credited with being the first to record the yews' unique growth pattern, the first to start an inventory of notable specimens and the first to open the debate as to their age and reason for planting.

In 1946 Vaughan Cornish followed up John Lowe's book, and his own work on historic thorn trees, with the publication *The Churchyard Yew and Immortality*. In his preface Vaughan Cornish stated that the reverence for the churchyard yew is rooted in pagan Britain and that the tree became incorporated into the Christian culture as 'an emblem of immortality'. He endorsed this view with the following seventeenth-century quote: 'Our forefathers were particularly careful in preserving churchyard yews that by reason of their perpetual verdue were emblematical of the immortality of the soul'. Vaughan Cornish also observed that Archbishops Lanfranc and Anselm came from northern Italy, where cypress had been planted in graveyards since Roman times, and that this may have influenced churchyard yew planting in Britain. He explored the use of yew foliage on Palm Sunday, and noted that in Ireland the yew was often called the 'palm' on account of its use in the processions on that day. Vaughan Cornish stated that the 'ancient' yews are mainly situated in the southern counties of England, and in *Britannia Secunda* 'the land beyond the Severn', most of which is now Wales. He listed the churchyard yews of the dioceses and parishes of England and Wales, and added that in Wales the tradition lingers that the yew is a symbol of immortality. Vaughan Cornish accepted an age range of 750 to 1000 years as reasonable for some of the oldest churchyard yews. His book is essential reading for students of the yew.

The most thorough study, exclusively devoted to one area of Wales, was undertaken by John Daryll Evans in his 1980s publication *The Churchyard Yews of Gwent* (1988). His greatest contribution to yew tree research was his view on the growth patterns of yew wood, and also the survey he undertook in the Gwent area of south Wales. The list he compiled included yews noted from old records, which had either been forgotten about or were now no longer in existence. These yews became known as 'lost' trees. Along with measurements to act as a guide to age, J. D. Evans' list has been used by later researchers as a useful data base for the significant yews of the Gwent region. Evans visited over 170 churchyards during 1986/7 and noted whether the sites had been places of worship from before the nineteenth century. He gave the circumference of the trunk, the position of the trees in their churchyard settings, and included notes of historical interest. Evans contributed to an ongoing debate about the age of old yews, siding with those who believed that the trees could attain thousands of years of age. He thought that the oldest yews were well in excess of 1000 years old. In the case of the Mamheilad yew he speculated that it might approach 3000 years of age. By holding this view he was suggesting that some yews predate Christianity by up to 1000 years. The basis of argument was built solely on tree measurement detail. In his work there was little analysis of pre-Christian or Christian history from the churchyard sites. His book makes a valuable contribution to the pool of knowledge of where old yews once grew and grow today. Of particular merit is his highlighting of the recent destruction of some old trees and his raising of the yews' profile in general churchyard study.

Prior to J. D. Evans' book, the only other study conducted in a particular region of Wales was J. Jones-Davies' survey of the yews around the county of Brecon, and sent out in a series of newsletters during 1970 by the Brecknock Museum Service as part of their contribution to European Conservation Year. Another local study inspired by both Evans and Jones-Davies is John Andrew's survey, conducted in the early 1990s, of the Gower peninsula churchyard yews.

On a wider perspective, and related to the age churchyard yews may attain and their reason for being planted, Oliver Rackham, writing in the 1980s, suggests that English churchyard yews could possibly live to be as old as an Anglo-Saxon church. However, he speculated that their true age and reason for planting remains a mystery. The late Alan Mitchell, influenced by Allen Meredith, talked of 2000 to 5000 year-old yews. In 1991 one of the more recent researchers, H. Hartzell, revisited the yews measured by de Candolle, Lowe and Cornish. He had the opinion that a 20-foot tree could be approximately 1400 years old, but that some trees may well be over 2000 years in age. Paul Tabbush and John White studied yew growth at different sites and produced papers estimating ages for open grown trees, and later for the woodland yews at Kingley Vale, Sussex. In 2000 T. R. Hindson produced a growth graph that shows yews that are potentially over 2000 years of age.

Donald Gregory devoted a chapter to yews in his 1991 historical study *Country Churchyards in Wales*. Amongst Gregory's observations were that yews were possibly planted near round barrows to indicate a supply of water. Gregory wrote that to the pagan, yew possessed magic properties and wands were made of yew. Gregory stated that the church bishops issued various edicts advising that old superstitions, such as tree and stone worship, should be treated with patience and understanding. As a result, according to Gregory, 'sacred' trees became tolerated by the clergy.

One of the lesser-known publications on the yew was written in 1992 by Trevor Baxter and titled *The Eternal Yew*. In the work Baxter explored historical and literary associations, and covered yews growing in the wild, in churchyards and on country estates. His most valuable contribution is the chapter on the unique growth pattern of the yew. His findings have a major part to play in understanding the difficulties of estimating the age of surviving trees, 'a perennial pastime for many dendrologists'. Although age estimates are being refined due to new techniques, in the absence of a reliable planting date estimates of age should be used as a guide. It seems obvious, but worth emphasising, that only a reliable planting date can give conclusive evidence of exact age. Baxter observed that many yews, but not all, develop more than one 'core point' within the trunk. Each one of these 'core points' starts a separate growth pattern that may in time result in a twin or multi-trunk appearance. These 'core points' may generate their own concentric ring growths. His key observation is that an all-enveloping circular ring on the periphery of the multiple or compound trunk continues to grow in a conventional way as though the new internal growth did not exist. Therefore the outward appearance of the trunk may show one unified stem, and centuries may pass before the trunk breaks out into separate stems. This growth pattern is observed fairly commonly, and yews growing in this manner develop a stout buttressed bole with a significantly increased girth at about 1.5 metres above ground level. Baxter gives photographic examples of sections of yew wood showing this pattern of growth.

Pests and diseases, subjects neglected by many, are covered in Baxter's book. The rotting of the yews' heartwood causes the hollowing of stems. This hollowing process can give an indication of the likely age of the yew. Many hollow trees have filled naturally with internal stems, or have man-made structures added such as seats, concrete, brickwork, even pulpits. Baxter's chapter on churchyard yews include the trees at Caerhun, Llanelltyd, Defynnog, and Gresford near Wrexham (*Wrecsam*). The Gresford yew is of particular interest as it has received much attention over the last 200 years, with various measurements having been taken by a variety of recorders. Of added interest is the discovery in 1902 of an early Christian stone, found during boiler house excavation work. Baxter's book raises important issues with regard to the growth patterns and estimated ages of yew trees in Britain. He concluded his publication with a list of notable yews taken from the Tree Register's database.

Allen Meredith, a tree enthusiast from Oxfordshire, had for some years been gathering information of ancient yew trees throughout the United Kingdom. His studies resulted in a work published in 1994 and written by Diana Brueton and Anand Chetan, entitled *The Sacred Yew*. This book contains much of the content explored in the works of John Lowe and Vaughan Cornish and it became popular with those attracted to things 'otherworldly'. To some readers a factual study took a back seat, but regardless of this Allen Meredith influenced some eminent botanists and arboriculturists who began to expand Meredith's thoughts on the international stage. Despite many drawbacks, the publication does explore more fully than previous studies the perceived 'Celtic' mythology of the yew.

An example of some of the dubious research contained in *The Sacred Yew* is the following extract: 'I think of the ancient yew of Fortingall, Perthshire, there when the megaliths were planted, the later Roman forts, the much later church...' It is quite a claim that a living tree could predate Bronze Age activity, Roman occupation, and the Christian period. There is no exploration of the work of the Irish saints in the fifth and sixth centuries in the Glen Lyon valley, the existence of secondary relics, or any possible connection with the planting of the yew at the site during that period. Working with the Conservation Foundation and drawing from different sources, Meredith established a database of ancient yews, which is set out in the back of *The Sacred Yew* publication. This gazetteer has a column devoted to age estimates and these range from 1000 to 5000 years old. This column has received the greatest attention and most controversy. Of the Welsh sites, Disgoed and Llangynyw have trees listed as 5000 years old, and Defynnog has a tree with an age estimate of more than 3000 years. There is more than one yew on this site, and Meredith states that a female tree and its close neighbour may be all part of the same tree. If so, it would be considerably the largest-girthed yew in the world. The book concludes with a list of 'lost' yews that until 'very recently' existed. Of the thirty-nine trees, eighteen are in Wales, including the Llanwrin churchyard yew, which, although cut severely in the mid 1980s, is not lost but has survived and regrown. There is little doubt that Allen Meredith's thoughts and data gave fresh attention to old yews. However, a question mark does remain over his age estimates.

In 2002 Robert Bevan-Jones' *The Ancient Yew* was published. In the preface to this detailed work is the observation that 'the yew is generally acknowledged as the British tree capable of longest life'. After a resumé of botanical features and techniques used for assessing age Bevan-Jones gives a chronological 'run-down' of students of the subject, including the work of H. A. Hyde, the author in 1931 of *Welsh Timber Trees*. Hyde queried the evidence available for 2000-year-old yews and took the view that several trunks could fuse together to create one trunk. Bevan-Jones devoted a separate section of his book to the churchyard yews of Wales. Its opening line reads: 'Wales probably has the largest collection of ancient yews in the world'. He went on to say that in Wales the concentration of churchyard yews per square kilometre is greater than in any other land. He covered the fragile state of some of the trees and the threat of fire damage to the hollow trunks of the 'ancients'. Bevan-Jones recognised that the past history of the churchyard yew is still 'imperfectly understood' but saw a continuous tradition of 1400 years of planting yews at places of burial and worship.

Bevan-Jones wrote about yews at abbey sites and covered in detail the yews past and present at the Strata Florida (*Ystrad Fflur*) monastic settlement. The visit of the meticulous travel writer Leland in the middle of the sixteenth century is the first recorded reference to yew trees on this site, and incidentally the only yews he recorded in his entire travel writing. George Borrow, on his tour of Wales in the 1870s, wrote of a yew tree at Strata Florida that stood just by the northern wall, and described the tree as being either split by lightning or by the force of wind. This yew was supposedly growing above the grave of the poet Dafydd ap Gwilym. Bevan-Jones argued convincingly that the tree now bearing the crude memorial stone and deemed to be Dafydd ap Gwilym's tree is not that which Borrow described, and that the much decayed and neglected old yew growing by the wall is the 'true' Dafydd ap Gwilym tree. As at Fountains Abbey, where ancient yews and a pre-Cistercian slab exist, Robert Bevan-Jones put forward the case that Strata Florida is in fact the site of an early saint's cell with associated 'spring' and yew trees. The lack of any recent detailed archaeological work cannot confirm this opinion. Whether the remaining yews are from an earlier period before the twelfth century is still to be proved (if indeed it can be). There would appear though to be some powerful circumstantial evidence in favour of the proposal. Bevan-Jones' book is thoroughly researched, containing new data and ideas and using the existing material to good effect. He readily stated that more evidence is required for accurate age estimates to be arrived at.

Contained within these reviewed works are references from other, mainly earlier publications. Literary sources for the yews of Wales are limited, so in order to fully evaluate the subject it has been necessary to study the research and records from the whole of Britain and Ireland. The question of the exact age of the oldest trees may never be answered, although a closer estimate can be found through a study of the sites on which they grow and by looking at the growth rates of trees with a known planting date.

Chapter Two

Botanical characteristics of *Taxus baccata*

Taxus baccata is variously referred to as the common yew, true yew, European yew or even as the English yew, but to my knowledge in Wales it is not known as the Welsh yew, only as 'the yew'. Despite these differing names it is however the same species and the similarities of the English and Welsh names Yew and Yw (ywen singular) respectively are so alike that it would seem that one was borrowed from the other. However after much research J Jones-Davies of Brecon came to the conclusion it was not possible to see which name came first. More importantly he was convinced that there must have been an early name for this tree that was common to all the old languages of Europe. The family to which the yew belongs, *Taxaceae*, spreads across the northern hemisphere and consists of six species, of which several are very similar. The Irish yew (*Taxus baccata 'fastigiata'*) found fairly commonly in churchyards, is an upright variety of the common yew. It was only 'discovered' in the early eighteenth century growing in the north of Ireland, so no offspring can be above 280 years old. *Taxus baccata* is native on chalk soils in southern England, and on limestone soils elsewhere. In Wales it can be found in oak woods on various soil types, and is particularly numerous in the vicinity of the Wye valley. It is probably generally more common now in Britain than in previous centuries. Almost pure stands of yew exist in southern England, the most notable example being Kingley Vale in Hampshire. The tree usually grows a broad crown, very often with a multi-stemmed bole. Old churchyard trees typically have a squat hollow trunk with much 'burring'. Another feature of old yews is a dense sprouting growth around the hollowed trunk. A commonly found distortion of the buds, appearing at the ends of the branches, is a growth named the 'artichoke gall'. It is caused by the yew gall midge (*Taxomyia taxi*). This abnormality does not harm the tree to any great extent, but in extreme cases it can retard growth.

The yew is classified as a dioecious species, meaning the tree is either male or female (except for some rare trees that have both male and female branches, eg. Llanerfyl and Abergwesyn). The male flowers are small, and are found beneath the undersides of the shoots of the previous year's growth. They become yellow and shed clouds of pollen in late February or early March. Female trees have minute single green flowers on which the arils swell into fleshy red 'fruits' from mid September onwards. These are the only non-poisonous parts of the tree and contain the hard seed that can become abundant in some autumns. They are feasted on by members of the thrush family, who digest the fleshy covering but pass the seed itself, so becoming the principal natural distributors of the species.

The foliage of the yew, when cut and withered, is particularly toxic and if eaten in quantity can kill both humans and livestock. There are historical reports of animals that have died after eating yew. For example, the vicar of Merthyr Cynog reported that in the severe winter of 1963 cattle entered his churchyard, and as a result of eating yew two cows died. However, green foliage growing on live trees is regularly browsed by both deer and livestock without undue effect, providing not too much is eaten at any one time. The common yew is recognised as a very long-lived tree with specimens possibly aged over 1000 years. The 'debate' as to what age these trees can attain still continues, with some experts taking the view that on religious sites some yews pre-date the current theological use. A more cautious view is that some yews can predate the existing buildings on ecclesiastical sites.

The wood of the common yew is distinctively pink-red in colour but the sapwood is paler in hue, and although the older trees can be hollow the wood is affected by very few pathogens. The main fungal infection that attacks the wood and starts the hollowing process is known as the 'sulphur fungus' (*Laetiporus sulphureus*). This creates a dry, brown, cubical heart-rot with a fruiting body that has a distinctive creamy yellow colouring, hence the '*sulphureus*'. The other two fungi that can attack the yew, but more rarely, are *Ganoderma lucidum* and *Ganoderma resinaceum*. Both these pathogens do limited damage to yew wood. Sometimes observed on any age of yew (as at Defynnog 2008) is a yellowing of needles on the previous year's growth, followed by their loss. This does not appear to cause death to the affected tree. The death of a whole yew tree is normally caused by the root-killing fungus *Phytophthora*.

Measuring and 'ageing' yews

The height and spread of a tree reaches an optimum size, and after a variable period of time starts to decrease. Neither height nor spread, then, will give an estimate of age except in a young tree. We are thus left with the circumference of the bole (or trunk) that must increase in some measure, no matter how small, every year of its life. The age of a tree, therefore, can be related to circumference alone when measuring takes place.

The internationally accepted method of measuring the girth of a tree is to position a metric tape on the 1.5 metre mark (measured from the highest point of the surrounding ground). On a clean, smooth, single trunk this is an easy operation. On old trees, particularly yews, this is not a straightforward task. The trunk can fork low and can consist of many stems below the measuring mark. The tree can have 'burrs', bumps or other growths, and hollows, which distort measurement. In these circumstances measurements should be taken at the narrowest point below 1.5 metres. In many cases this may be at, or close to, ground level. This uncertainty of measurement creates great scope for potential error and confusion: for example, have all measurers used the same point of measurement? The results over several centuries by different measurers have produced conflicting records that cannot be relied upon, and from which growth or age predictions become meaningless. Added to this, some of the biggest old yews are unmeasurable at any point due to split or broken trunks and missing limbs (eg. Llandre, Llandrillo). Also yew wood, as previously described, can develop unusual and 'chaotic' growth patterns. Stems often grow together, with the outer bark surrounding the 'multi-stemming' and appearing to suggest one single stem or branch. In such cases, the measurement of trees can lead to misleading calculations on possible age. Only by systematic measuring, preferably on smooth-boled young trees, or trees where measurements have taken place at the same point, and ideally by the same person, over a period of years, can patterns of growth related to age produce a reliable graph. The difficulties described above lead one to the view that girth measurements of 'ancient yews' can only be used as a very rough guide.

Therefore, a number of key features, such as hollowing and decay, fragmentary remains, plus girth measurement, and also (it could be argued) the age of the site on which the tree grows, give us the confidence to give a yew the title 'ancient'.

Other methods of ageing trees are carbon dating and dendrochronology, the results of which are used to determine a pattern for the accurate dating of a given piece of wood. The problem with many yew trees is that because of the hollowing process the oldest part of the tree no longer exists, so there is no material to test or examine. However, both carbon dating and dendrochronology can give some indication of possible age, and radio-carbon dating has been carried out on at least two yews, Loughton in Shropshire and Overton near Wrexham.

Historical usage of yew

The oldest wooden implement so far discovered worldwide is a spearhead made of yew, found at the Clacton-on-Sea archaeological dig in Essex in 1969. This dig revealed tools from the Lower Palaeolithic Occupation of Britain. According to Professor Lloyd Laing of Nottingham University, the spearhead is dated at approximately 250,000 years old. Another weapon, found on the Somerset Levels, is the Meare Heath yew bow, dated to 3500 BC. It measures almost 2 metres in length and was capable of shooting an arrow over 100 metres. The bow is similar to the medieval longbows used with great effect against the French troops at the battle of Agincourt in 1415 AD.

Yew wood has been used for many artefacts over the centuries. The small Romano-British decorative head that was found at the Roman camp near Llanio in Ceredigion, in the nineteenth century was probably used as a form of 'protection' against evil spirits. One of the most beautiful ecclesiastical uses of yew-wood is displayed in Boher church, near Lemanaghan, in central Ireland: the reliquary case of St Manchan dating from the early twelfth century is the largest and most magnificent shrine to have been found in either Ireland or Britain, and has cast gilt bronze and red fittings fixed onto a tent-shaped frame of yew wood. Another example is the crozier of a ninth-century Irish bishop, the staff of which was made from yew (British Museum).

A more recent usage of yew is in medical science, where the beneficial effects of the foliage of the *Taxus* species is at present receiving extensive trialling in cancer research.

To conclude, it is fair to say that yew has an extremely long association with humankind, both in a beneficial and a potentially harmful way. This association may well be why the species has appeared to hold a special place within the folk culture of Britain and Ireland over many centuries.

Chapter Three

Trees in Pre-Christian and Christian History

In early Iron Age Britain the larger communities may have had a form of 'priest' who managed religious activity and gave guidance and advice to the local population. However, the idea that a universal and uniform Druidic religion existed seems unlikely until the later stages of that period. It is more likely that a few core religious beliefs were common to all the regions of Britain and they came out of, and were developed from, earlier ideologies from the distant past. The archaeologist Francis Pryor suggests that in the early Iron Age the 'rites' in the regions would have been as diverse as the communities that practised them. It is therefore difficult, when considering tree worship, to give hard and fast rules as to common practice, let alone determine which species held particular reverence.

In the early post-Roman period the veneration of trees played a major part in Anglo-Saxon pagan religious practices and the yew may have attracted various superstitions, through the Saxons' contact with neighbouring Celts. Every culture is influenced to some degree by those it has contact with, and this could explain the presence of 'ancient' yews in Saxon churchyards throughout southern England and the Welsh border counties with Wales. The Celts of mainland Europe are believed to have cut ogham characters onto yew 'wands', and it is possible that this made the wood of yew extra special, for it became linked with runes, the 'magic' letters that, it was believed, could repel evil. Recent excavations in Saxon Frisia have revealed two possible amulets made from yew with runic inscriptions on them. There are, though, those who see no particular historical evidence for the yew holding an elevated position above the other native tree species of Britain. The sparsity of place names containing the element 'yew' does not give particular encouragement to the view that the yew held the status of a 'special' tree. However, surely the mere presence of the old churchyard 'ancients' elevates them to having some form of connection, either culturally or practically, with the sites on which they grow.

The nature writer Richard Mabey notes in his seminal work *Flora Britannica* that yews of great age are rarely found outside churchyards, and that he is not aware of any other similarly exclusive relationship between places of worship and a single tree species existing anywhere else in the western world.

Work on the history of the parish boundaries surrounding Offa's Dyke raises questions about churchyard yews and Saxon settlements. Assuming that existing parishes dissected by Offa's Dyke were established by the eighth century, the very fact that the Dyke cuts across these parishes indicates that the earthwork was imposed upon existing earlier administrative areas. The early Saxon settlements from before the time of King Offa include Casgob and Buttington. The churchyards in both these locations have yews of significant size and age. The question is who planted the yews in those settlements – the early Saxons or the native population – or were the yews planted after the construction of the Dyke?

If we go back further in history and explore the association between the yew and the Celts, we find that Irish sources produce some interesting evidence. The influence of Ireland on Christianity in Wales and Britain as a whole, and vice versa, is well documented. Therefore researching Irish 'sacred trees' may cast some light on the subject in Wales.

In Ireland it was fairly common practice to carry pieces of wood or bark from a sacred or holy tree as a form of protection. This custom has its origins in the pagan past, as does touching wood to bring good luck is today (reference to Saxon Frisia amulets above). The seventh- or eighth-century Irish law text *Bretha Comaithchesa* contains a list of twenty-eight trees and shrubs divided into four classes, of which the highest class of seven 'noble' species lists *Ibair* (yew) amongst its most important trees. The sacredness of a tree – not exclusively, but very often, yew – is explained by association with a particular saint who is said to have either lived beside or founded a church near a special tree. In some cases a 'planted' staff 'became' the special tree: the staff invariably took root when stuck in the ground. This 'miracle' is also common in Saxon folklore, for example Congar's Stick from Congresbury in Somerset, and St Bertram's Stick from Ilam in Staffordshire, the latter recorded as still growing in 1686. This particular tree grew above a spring: echoes here with some Irish sacred ash trees such as St Manchan's Tree and Well in County Offaly, Ireland. It was considered a bad omen to break a bough off St Bertram's sacred tree.

Other examples of saints' trees in Saxon England that sprouted from staffs are those of Cynhelm, Eadwold, Aldhelm and Oswald. An Irish 'staff' tree named after St Moling (*Crann Moling*) grew near Inistioge in Co. Kilkenny. St Moling had a hermitage nearby and there is a spring near the site where a holy yew once grew. The altar, which once faced the original yew, is still covered with stones, statues, crosses and other votive offerings. Although a tree still stands on the site, *Crann Moling* cannot be the actual tree where Moling worshipped in the seventh century, but it continues a strong custom.

The tradition of sacred trees is older than Christianity and common to many religions and cultures. For example, the Ancient Greeks regarded trees as the first temples of the gods; the Egyptian sacred tree stood on the threshold of life and death. The bo-tree, at Anuradhapura in Sri Lanka has been the centre of Buddhist ceremonies since time immemorial, and the Hindu banyan tree is seen as the 'Cosmic Tree' of life. Arunta tribal celebrations in Australia revolve around the sacred pole, in the Q'uran the tree symbol is a powerful force, and the great 'Angel oak' in South Carolina is believed to be haunted by the souls of the slaves.

Trees in the Bible

In the Hebrew Bible tree association is very evident. In Genesis we are told that 'Abraham prayed under a tamarisk tree, by the well of Beersheba' (Gen.18: 4) and in Exodus we read of God appearing to Moses in a flame of fire out of a bush on the side of Mount Horeb (Ex. 3:2-4). Trees were associated with Kingship and there is an example of an inauguration tree in Judges, 'the oak that stood in Sichem' in the story of Ahimelech's coronation (Judges 9:6-15). Also in Judges there are references to the olive, fig, vine, bramble and cedar (Judges 9:8-16). Some other biblical tree references are: 'and she sat under a palm tree, which was called by her name, between Rama and Bethel in Mount Ephraim, and the children of Israel came up to her for all judgement' (Judges 4:5), and also from Judges: 'one troop cometh by the way that looketh towards the oak' (Judges 9:37). In Isaiah we find 'the rod from the root of Jesse' (Is. 11.1), and from the Prophecy of Jeremias, the Messiah was to be the scion of David, 'a just branch' (Jer. 23:5). In Ezekiel we are told that 'the Assyrian was like a cedar of Libanus' (Ezek. 31:3-18), and in Daniel there is the description of the 'great and strong' tree (Dan. 4:7-17). Yet another biblical tree reference is found in Zacharias, 'In that day, said the Lord of hosts, every man shall call his friend under the vine and under the fig tree' (Zach. 3:10), and in chapter four there is reference to two olive trees 'on the right side of the candlestick', which are described as 'the two sons of oil' (Zach. 4:11-14).

Probably the most widely quoted passage with tree associations from the New Testament relates to Jesus' entry into Jerusalem accompanied by 'the cutting and strewing of boughs' (Matthew. 21:8) and the 'taking branches of palm trees' (John 12:13). Interpretations relating to this last passage are dealt with later.

Trees in Irish literature

The theme of the association of kingship and trees is evident in the Irish saga *Dindshenchas* with a line that reads: 'Behind them is a high hill, and on it is the shining tree'. At the important monastery at Kells could be found 'the great oak tree'. With reference to a holy yew, St Patrick was credited with planting one known as the 'Bile of Swords' (the word 'bile' (plural 'bileda') refers to a sacred or venerated tree). Also from the 'Book of Armagh' (tenth century) it is written that St Patrick built his first church for the priest Justanus beside Bile Tortan, widely believed to be a yew tree.

One of the clearest insights into the position a holy yew could hold in early Christian Ireland appears in the following ninth-century poem, from *Sages, Saints and Storytellers*:

> There is here above the host
> A tall bright glistening yew
> A sweet bell sends out a clear note
> In the church of Colum, descendent [sic] of Níall.

The great Celtic theologian Adomnán, abbot of Iona and chronicler on the life of St Columba, showed his awareness of the biblical tradition of the 'holy tree' in his acclaimed seventh-century explanation of the scriptures, *De Locis Sanctis*. He describes the hill of Mamre, near Hebron, where stood the oak of Mamre or Abraham's Oak, 'because once upon a time he entertained angels under it'. The oak was twice the height of a man and enclosed in a church. In a story familiar in medieval Ireland, Muirchú describes an event in which an angel speaks to Patrick out of a burning bush, '... but it did not burn down, as had happened to Moses before'. In parts of the Irish tradition the tree almost becomes a sacred being in its own right. The Yew of Ross, for example, was one of the great legendary trees of ancient Ireland and had a 'litany' composed in its honour. The 'litany' of the Yew of Ross (*Eó Rossa*) appears in the twelfth-century *Book of Leinster*. Like many items of folklore, it is probably based on older material and both the 'Lives' (hagiographies) of Molaise and Moling describe the tree's downfall during the early part of the seventh century.

An example of the superstitions associated with any wilful damage carried out on sacred trees appears in the writings of the chronicler Giraldus Cambrensis (Gerald of Wales). He wrote in his twelfth-century *Topographia Hibernia* that a group of Anglo-Norman archers became smitten with pestilence 'in retribution for their impiety' after they had cut down the yews and ash trees at the monastery at Finglas. The yew in the tale 'The Yew of the Disputing Sons' has mysterious 'otherworld' properties, for it could give shelter for up to 300 warriors and could give protection against all dangers. It could also become an apparition and could 'fell' warriors due to its deadly qualities described in the text as 'the venom of the russet-bowed yew'. The poisonous nature of the species was obviously well known, confirmed by the plant knowledge appearing in Cormac Mac Culennain's work *Bretha Comaithchesa*, which lists yew as a potential killer of livestock. The old tales are probably only the fragmentary remains of a once much larger corpus of ancient tree-lore from the Celtic past.

A good reference to the role of a saint's yew is seen in the poem contained in the Irish work *Betha Choluim Chille*. The translation reads: 'When I entered into the Black Church: and in especial above [*sic*] in the yew tree in front of the Black Church, where Columcille [Columba] and his saints were wont to chant the hours, were there ten thousand angels keeping guard, as Columcille hath said in these quatrains:

This is the yew of the Saints
Where they used to come with me together
Ten hundred angels were there
Above our heads, side close by side.
Dear to me is that yew tree;
Would that I were set in its place there!
On my left it was pleasant adornment.'

This is a clear unambiguous reference to a saintly yew. The work was by O'Donnell in 1532, but it follows the biographical lines of the Old Irish 'Life', adding materials from other sources including Adomnán. It is mixed with local legends and ancient poems to create the whole.

Another poetic reference to churchyard yews comes in the exploits of the legendary Mad Sweeney (*Suibhne Geilt*) who, tradition relates, was the king of *Dál Riata* during the seventh century. The sixth verse reads:

The yew tree in each churchyard
Wraps night in its dark hood.
Ivy is a shadowy
Genius in the wood

This early poem gives another clear indication of the accepted tradition of yew and holy place.

A curious mixture of the pagan and Christian is in evidence in the tale 'The Exile of Conal Corc'. This eighth- or ninth-century text describes a yew growing on a prominent stone in front of a small oratory. The druid of Aed declares that 'whomsoever kindles a fire under the yew, from him shall descend the kingship of Munster'. This can be interpreted as how an ancient royal site gets the approval of a druid to its 'new' Christian presence. The inclusion of 'fire' in the poem echoes Brigid's eternal fire at Kildare, a site with strong tree associations.

A. T. Lucas, in his 1963 paper on the 'Sacred Trees of Ireland', gives references to church sites and place names associated with yew trees. This evidence, although not from Wales, clearly shows the important role that trees, particularly yew, had in the period of conversion. This applied to both the adoption of sites and modification of beliefs. However, caution is required, for the yews planted in the Christian period were the trees of the Christians and not 'pagan trees'. The early texts tell us, then, that the Irish influence on Wales and vice versa contributed to the importance placed on the yew tree in both those lands. 'Saints' yews' appear to be a feature, common to both, in the early to middle medieval period.

Some of the earliest ecclesiastical foundations (e.g. at Clonmacnois) were deliberately sited at pagan places where there existed sacred groves and trees. The Church then introduced Christian ritual at these sites and, as Lewis puts it, 'the church came to the tree, not the tree to the church'. The bond between tree and church grew, culminating in trees coming to the churches and associated saints, with deliberate planting taking place within the holy enclosure. The sacred qualities of the ancestral tree survived. Any self-sown seedlings growing up within the protected confines of the ecclesiastical site would eventually be accorded the same reverence as other sacred trees. The importance of sacred trees acting as guardians at Christian sites can be illustrated by the references in the Irish annals to St Cíarán's Yew at Clonmacnois and the 'Bile of Swords'growing at the lost monastery of Iubhar chinntrechta (a yew is mentioned in this place name). These trees were struck by lightning and destroyed, but in so being they preserved the adjacent buildings from damage. The sacred tree acted as a protector of the holy enclosure.

By the time Giraldus Cambrensis toured Ireland there is a different story to tell of the yew trees of the 'sacred places'. After his tour in 1184 he noted that yews with 'their bitter sap' were more frequently to be found in Ireland than in any other country he had visited, but '... you see them principally in old cemeteries and sacred places, where they were planted in ancient times by the hands of holy men, to give them what ornament and beauty they could, for now we see many of them broken down and trampled'. His description of the yews is either an accurate portrait of declining and neglected trees or merely a good assessment of ancient specimens. Whatever he observed is now gone, and that remains one of the greatest mysteries of yew tree research. His comment about beauty and ornament seems to have understated the role the yew really played in early medieval Ireland.

Yews in Welsh literature and legend

Yew references from early Welsh literature and folklore sources are less easy to find than in Irish writing. This is maybe not surprising as there is less of a corpus of work to explore anyway. There are, though, two significant references worth quoting in some depth. The first is taken from *Liber Landavensis, Llyfr Teilo: Ancient Register of the Cathedral of Llan-daf* (otherwise known as 'The Book of Llandaf') under the heading 'The Village of Miluc'. Miluc is an unidentifiable place now, although some clues exist as to its whereabouts. It is known for example that it was near the river Ely (*Afon Elái*) in Glamorgan. J. R. Davies has suggested the site is possibly Garth Maelwg but it is probably located nearer to Llandaf. The text tells us that Iestyn sent his 'household', containing the wicked Twrwerd and Iestyn's grandson Eineon, 'filled with an evil spirit' to Llandaf. Ignoring the protection of the holy cross and the asylum given by the Llandaf saints of St Dubricius, St Teilo and St Oudoceus, the sinners 'took away a virgin who had fled under the protection of the church, and from between the yewtree and the church'. (The Latin text reads thus '… *episcope rapuerunt uiginem de fubala ecclesie aufugentem infra taxum et ecclesiam*'.) The story continues that the girl, Eurddilad daughter of Cynwal, was 'violated' and that the perpetrator became deranged. The Bishop cursed Iestyn and his criminals for such an outrage. Intriguingly the punishment was for violation of the protected 'refuge', not for the rape of the maiden.

Eventually Iestyn acknowledged that he had acted improperly towards 'God and his Pastor' and sought pardon. The violated maiden was restored, and Iestyn gave the village of Miluc back to God and the saints. No payment was to be paid to any man other than to the Church of Llandaf. There is then in the text a list of clergy and laity who acted as witnesses, and a description of the land-holding of the village and environs affected by the agreement. Although not actually stating that the yew was acting as a 'protector' in its own right, there would appear to be an inference that that area between the church and yew tree was a sacred space or 'special refuge'. What also seems apparent is the acceptance of the yew as an integral part of the site or *llan*.

Also from the 'Book of Llandaf' are several other tree references associated with land boundaries, including one under the heading of 'The Church of Dincat'. The description reads: '… along the brook to a ditch on the left in the direction of the Trothy, to a small brook, and along it to the Trothy, to a Yewtree ford on the Trothy, through the Trothy along the ditch upwards, along the brook to its source'. Chapter 10 refers to Ystradyw, an ancient district of southern Breconshire, probably taking its name from the river Ywen, which flows through the area. Here the word 'yw' is contained in the place name. However the Miluc yew reference is unique as it is not associated with specific boundary descriptions. Although treated with caution by scholars for its political bias, the 'Book of Llandaf' is seen as a valuable resource from the medieval period in Wales. It is thought to date from before the death of Bishop Urban, the last bishop of Llandaf, who died in 1133.

The second important reference occurs in *The Laws of Hywel Dda* and is assumed to have originated in the tenth century. This early dating is based on the observation that some passages, found in comparatively later manuscripts, are so archaic in substance and language that they must pre-date Hywel's time. Some of the phrases and passages may have been transmitted orally, but others appear too complicated for that, especially when knowing that medieval Welsh legal practice laid great emphasis on written statements of law. Further evidence for early influence can be read in the Introduction, which states that the Welsh law books, on which the translation is based, were produced by, or for, lawyers between the early thirteenth and early sixteenth centuries, but significantly it is emphasised that their foundation is a small core of material from around the middle of the tenth century. That material was put together 'under the auspices of Hywel Dda'. There are similarities within Hywel's Law to early Irish law manuscripts, suggesting an origin from a common Celtic social source. In Chapter Five monetary values are placed against various species of tree. The tree with the greatest value is a 'holy' or 'saint's' or 'consecrated' yew (depending on translation) with a value of one pound, compared to fifteen pence for a woodland yew and thirty pence for an ordinary or 'secular' yew. The importance of this item of 'law' is the greater value placed on a 'holy' yew than on all other tree species, including a 'secular' yew. Also this early medieval reference provides evidence that these special category yews were growing in the churchyards of that period.

Liturgical use of yew

The use of yew foliage for various liturgical practices is alluded to in both written and verbal history. Palm Sunday, the sixth Sunday of Lent, is recorded as a special holy day in Spain and Gaul from around 600 AD onwards. The blessing of palm branches on Palm Sunday is attested in Europe from around the middle of the eighth century. According to Aelfric's Catholic Homilies 'the priest shall bless palm twigs on this day and distribute them'. Even so, early European records do not mention any carrying of branches, unlike in the east where, from the fifth century onwards in Jerusalem, a procession of palm or olive branches took place following a liturgy of the word.

In Europe after the eighth century the practice of a 'palm' procession spread, but because of the unavailability of palm and olive the blessing of other 'green and blossoming branches' occurred. The substitute species used depended on what was green during the Lenten period. Fresh willow was used in some regions (and still is in central and eastern Europe), and the yew, which is 'evergreen' – as are both olive and palm – was used elsewhere, particularly in those areas of Britain and Ireland where the yew grew as a native plant. Yew foliage then began to develop an important role in the ritual practices surrounding Palm Sunday.

The earliest English reference to the rite of entry into penance on Ash Wednesday is recorded in the Leofric Missal in the late ninth century. However, it is probable that it was adopted by the Anglo-Saxon and Celtic churches as early as the seventh or eighth centuries. Clerics and laymen had ashes sprinkled on their heads, while women had a sign of the cross made with ashes on their foreheads, and from the eleventh century onwards a special prayer for the blessing of the ashes was introduced. The ashes, which according to the new Missal should be taken from the blessed 'palm' branches from the preceding year, are then sprinkled with holy water and distributed.

So here is a two-fold liturgical use for yew foliage, and by having a special yew growing in the churchyard a ready supply of available material was at hand. In fact it is expanded further, for the protective element of wearing a sprig of yew to bring 'good fortune' from Palm Sunday until Easter Day was recorded by the Rev. Johns in nineteenth-century Ireland. The practice continued until the late twentieth century and is recalled by many country folk.

Further endorsements for the use of yew foliage on Palm Sunday follow. William Caxton in the fifteenth century wrote 'Wherefore Holy Chirche this day makyth solemn processyon, in memory of the processyon that Cryst made this day. But for the euchson that we have none Olyve that bereth grene leef, algate therefore we take Ewe instead of palm and olyve, and beren about in processyon, and so is thys day called Palm Sunday.' There is an entry in a Churchwardens' Accounts of 1524 for payment 'for yew foliage'. It can be assumed that the foliage was used on Palm Sunday. The publication *Notes and Queries* has the following extract:

> the church has, from the earliest period, held this day the highest respect. Among our superstitious forefathers the palm-tree or it substitutes, box or yew, were solemnly blessed, and some of their branches burnt to ashes and used by the priests on the Ash Wednesday the following year, while other boughs were gathered and distributed amongst the pious, who bore them about in numerous processions.

The seventeenth-century poet Henry Vaughan, buried at Llantsantffraid-on-Usk, knew the yew tree as 'the palm' and wrote a poem about its qualities in 1655. Extracts from the 'Palm Tree' in *Silex Scintillans* are as follows:

> A tree ne'r to be priced,
> A tree whose fruit is immortality …

and the conclusion to the poem reads:

> To pluck a Garland hence, while you do sleep,
> and weave it for your head against you wake.

Milton, too, referred to the yew as 'the branching palm'. Recorded from Devon in 1775 is the note 'That a yew or palm-tree was planted in the churchyard, ye south side of the church, in the same place where one was blown down by the wind a few days ago, this 25th November'. John Lowe also confirmed that in east Kent churchyard yews were referred to as 'palms' as late as the end of the nineteenth century.

The role of the yew in burial ceremony is an elusive one for which little documentary evidence exists. However, I witnessed a sprig of yew being placed into a freshly dug grave in a remote Welsh churchyard in the mid 1980s. When the gravedigger was questioned he offered the explanation: 'It is customary, and would wish a good passing to the deceased.'

There is a general reference by Ablett from the late nineteenth century to the old custom of the carrying of yew branches over the dead by mourners at a funeral. The branches were then thrown beneath the coffin into the grave. Included in Rev. Johns' account of the yew in 1860 is the historian Martyn's quote that 'Our forefathers were particularly careful to preserve this funereal tree, whose branches it was usual to carry in solemn procession to the grave and afterwards to deposit therein under the bodies of their departed friends'. Added credence to the practice appears in Shakespeare's *Twelfth Night* where in Act Two the clown sings: 'My shroud of white, stuck all with yew, O prepare it, My part of death, no one so true, Did share it'.

Also from the seventeenth century Thomas Stanley, writer and poet, gives another glimpse of death and the yew:

> Yet strew, Upon my grave, Such offerings you have,
> Foresaken cypresse and sad Ewe,
> For kinder flowers can take no birth,
> Or growth from such unhappy earth.

From a later century A. E. Houseman (1897-1936) wrote in his famous poem *A Shropshire Lad*:

> Bring in this timeless grave to throw,
> No Cypress, sombre on the snow;
> Snap not from the bitter yew,
> His leaves that live December through ...

A similar theme was explored in *The Gentlemans Magazine* of 1781 where it was suggested that in pagan Greek and Roman civilisations the displaying of cypress and yew branches was a signal of a house in mourning. A question to be asked here is whether the foliage was a symbol of death, or truimph over death, due in part to the evergreen nature or 'perpetual verdure' of the foliage.

John Lowe refers to Roman funeral rites and the use of cypress and pine being replaced in Britain by yew foliage, as 'the other species were not available to them'. In J Jones-Davies' 1970 survey of the yews of the Brecon region he makes reference to gravestone inscriptions that reads in Welsh; *'gorwe'dd dan yr Ywen'* translated as 'sleeping under the yew' and *'Tan yr Ywen las ganghennog Dwmpath gwyrddlas cwyd dy ben'* ('under the green leafed branching yew, grassy mound, raise your head'). This last inscription describes the mounding present around the base of many churchyard yews probably created by the earthing up process when graves have been dug nearby.

Yews then could be used for differing purposes throughout the liturgical year. The foliage could adorn the church during festival periods and it was used as a vital part of both Ash Wednesday and Palm Sunday activity. Eventually the foliage adopted special protective powers, so adding to its already elevated status. It played an important role in funerary ritual, taking on special symbolism associated with resurrection and protection, probably brought about by the evergreen nature of the species. The amalgamation of both usefulness and symbolism made the yew an integral part of the sacred space.

Other possible reasons for the planting of yews in Welsh churchyards

Further encouragement for the cultivation of the churchyard yew was given by Edward I (1272-1307) who, after overcoming Llywelyn, instigated a series of directives that included his determination to establish the ownership of churchyard trees. Yews were by then an established feature of churchyards, and Edward indicated that one reason they occurred in churchyards was to defend the church buildings from high winds. He approved of more planting, but instructed that if the trees proved an obstruction to any repairs necessary to the chancels they should be cut down. Lowe, though, describes Edward's Statute 35 churchyard references as merely a repetition of what had originally appeared in the Magna Carta in 1215.

The growing of yews for the supply of suitable bow wood is a popular interpretation of why they were planted in protected churchyards. The skill of the Welsh bowmen in military history is commonly quoted. However, it is hard to find factual evidence to support the theory that the primary purpose for the planting of yews in churchyards was for archery purposes. Hansard's classic work on archery gives a number of reasons why the theory does not sound convincing, the first of which is piety, for, he says, there would have been considerable opposition to the cutting of wood grown on consecrated ground.

More convincing, perhaps, is the case that most churchyard yews are totally unsuitable in their growth pattern for the production of good bow wood, being both 'knotty' and crooked. Hansard judged that even by the most optimistic calculations the churchyards could not have supplied anywhere near the amount of wood necessary to have met the considerable military demands. In the fifteenth century Richard III's 1483 enactment allowed both for the planting and protecting of yew trees for their use by archers, which at that time gave some limited impetus to the churchyard/archery connection. The enactment was not specific to churchyard trees, but from the Elizabethan era we read that yews should be planted in churchyards and cemeteries – partly to ensure their cultivation and protection but also to prevent their leaves from injuring cattle.

Although not the original or primary reason for the occurrence of the yew in churchyards, these later uses acted as a stimulus for continued planting and maintenance, and made sure that the yew will always be identified as the tree of the country churchyard and cemetery.

Chapter Four

The History of the Early Church in Wales

Almost all the 'ancient' yews of Wales grow in churchyards. Therefore in order to explore their background and to assess their likely age and possible reasons for planting, it is necessary to look at the history of the early Welsh church. This is not a straightforward task, as was recognised by Wendy Davies who, in 1982, stated that the archaeology of the early church in Wales had received little attention compared with many other parts of Britain and Ireland. She gave the reason for this as the lack of documentary sources. However, the inscribed memorials, cross-marked stones and carved crosses found in Wales give clues as to some of the early history. The presence of an inscribed stone is seen as a good indicator of the antiquity of a site, but as some were moved into churches and churchyards from the surrounding countryside for safe keeping, care needs to be taken in assuming the site is automatically an early medieval one. It is likely that the formula used for the inscriptions on the stones was introduced into western Britain from western France in the mid to late fifth century. However, can the inscribed stones without any obvious Christian symbols be assumed to be necessarily Christian? Also what is their association, if any, with burials, and do they have any relationship to important routeways and boundaries? The inscribed stone at Llanerfyl in central Wales poses such questions. Apart from the early Christian stone monuments there are very few surviving artefacts that might give clues to the early origins of churchyards. There are eight saints' hand-bells existing in Wales, and fragments survive from the shrine of Gwenfrewi, originally held at Gwytherin in Denbighshire. The shrine would have originally held either the partial remains or the secondary relics of the local saint, and their existence emphasises the importance of such material, not only for the early Irish church but for the Welsh church too.

Pioneer work was done by the historical geographer E G Bowen in the second half of the twentieth century. He sought to trace the origins of the early Welsh church by studying the distribution of the 'Celtic' or local saints' dedications. Whilst recognising the importance of this work in bringing attention to the subject, more recent studies have queried some of Bowen's conclusions. However, there appears to be broad agreement that Bowen's ideas on the location of church sites and the relevance of dedications is still of value to the modern researcher.

Following on from Bowen's distribution maps, John Reuben Davies observes that the occurrence of a *llan* site (holy enclosure) with the addition of a name probably signifies an early medieval origin. He strongly indicates that local saints had begun to be a part of Welsh place-names, or were being associated with ecclesiastical sites no later than the end of the seventh century. Despite the lack of clarity he feels that the process of linking *llan* to a saint to create a compound name, if started by the end of the seventh century, had died out by the middle of the eleventh. Further to this, *'llan'* became understood to be a 'church-complex' with a defined cemetery for lay burial. This was likely to be a pattern of the eighth and ninth centuries, and it was within those 200 years and the following century that the main *llan* + saint names were established. Major cult saints such as David and Illtud probably dated from the sixth century, but dedications of today's churches can be misleading, as they may well be re-dedications from a later date. Their cults, however, probably commenced soon after their death. Other famous sixth-century saints such as Teilo and Cadog left evidence of their main churches and the memorials of their 'relics'. The names of 'obscure saints' probably indicate early names of sixth- or seventh-century provenance, but there is difficulty in confirming this. The cults of these saints lacked the means to expand, so they remained extremely localised.

An interesting example of the early Irish influence in Wales is the occurrence of the place name Llansanffraid, a place name associated with the cult of the Irish St Brigid. At Llansantfraid in Elvel (*Llansanffraid yn Elfael*) churchyard in Radnorshire grows an impressive collection of old yews. There is also an old yew of note at Llansantffraid juxta Usk. A scenario then can be imagined where foundations associated with certain 'holy men/holy women' in the sixth and early seventh centuries continued to develop after their death. Their 'remains' or 'relics' were then venerated and the site came to be called after them via a place-name. Some of the prominent 'holy men' had widespread cults usually associated with royal dynasties and political power. In the late tenth and first half of the eleventh century a changing political scene and attacks by Vikings adversely affected the interest in these native cults. However, by the end of the eleventh century there was fresh interest in this 'cult of the saints'. This culminated in new building and rebuilding of churches followed by rededications to the native saints of the old era. The hagiographers (saints' biographers) played a major role in creating and stimulating the profile of these saint's cults. However, despite the advances in our knowledge of the early period of Welsh ecclesiastical history, J. R. Davies emphasises that Wales' past was not conveniently written down for us to check all the details, so the task of working back through history to the 'age of the Welsh saints' is not an easy one.

As well as Welsh place-names shedding light on the possible antiquity of a site, descriptive words also give indications of antiquity and usage. An example of an early Welsh word that alludes to a holy place where the physical remains of a martyr could be found is *Merthyr*, which is the translation of the Latin *martyrium*. Coincidentally, Merthyr Cynog churchyard in Breconshire has impressive old yews.

Clasau (mother churches) were sites headed by abbots or abbesses, especially where there were dual communities – both male and female Christian communities co-existing alongside each other. These establishments existed in Welsh areas that were predominately controlled by the native population. They are seen as being traceable back to the pre-Norman period. The sites themselves, however, may have originated in an earlier period altogether, and studies on the shapes and sizes of *llan* show the probable antiquity of curvilinear churchyard enclosures. Larger enclosures could signify particularly important ritual sites and/or sacred places. An example of such a site, confirmed as being used in the Bronze Age, is Pennant Melangell at the head of the

Tanat valley in Montgomeryshire.

A study by Heather James of early Christian sites in the area of mid and south Wales close to either side of the English–Welsh border concludes that after taking into account such factors as place-names and dedications, three-quarters of the largely curved sites are likely to be pre-Norman; also that sites dating back to before the ninth century and having large enclosures probably represent the high status church *llannau*. Two good examples are the Breconshire sites of Llanafan Fawr and Defynnog that both contain early Christian inscriptions. Significantly both of these sites have yew trees that are amongst the largest and probably the oldest in Wales. Another site from Breconshire with a large curved yard is Merthyr Cynog, which as previously stated contains within its boundary significant yew trees. Similar sites from the study area with big old yews are Nantmel and Cascob (*Casgob*). Half of the earliest churchyards west of Offa's Dyke and known to exist before the ninth century have curvilinear boundaries.

As stated previously it is unfortunate that in Wales there have been few churchyard enclosures that have had extensive excavation. Of those that have, the Capel Maelog site near Llandrindod Wells provides a start date of construction no earlier than mid eighth century and completed in pre-Conquest times. The excavation at Burry Holms has identified the site as a likely hermitage with two phases of building, both of them pre-dating the existing twelfth-century church. Despite the paucity of excavations, the work at Pennant Melangell shows an enclosure that had funerary activity taking place within its boundaries as far back as the middle Bronze Age. However, it is generally agreed that more archaeological work from a range of sites is needed before we can be more confident about the continuity of usage of churchyard enclosures.

It is the majority opinion that church development in Wales started with a cemetery enclosure or *llan*. On some of these sites timber shrines were built, and on the more important sites they would have also had oratories. Either simple timber and then stone churches would have succeeded these, or they developed straight from the wooden oratory to a basic stone-built church. This development occurred during the late sixth or seventh centuries, but not all sites eventually had a church located on the site. Some sites stopped developing at given points in time for a number of differing reasons.

More recent thought is not as definite or as certain about the ancient origins of all the curvilinear churchyards. Some may have been more recent creations and not necessarily early cemeteries at all. The work on early medieval cemeteries in Wales revealed that the number of Iron Age enclosures that were used as early cemeteries could be increased if you include those that contained early Christian inscribed stones: this is assuming that these stones were grave markers.

One of the problems in Wales is the lack of surviving early structures – unlike in England, where there are good examples of Anglo-Saxon church buildings. Wales has only one surviving piece of a pre-Norman church and that is near the English border at Presteigne in Radnorshire. During the twelfth century many stone churches were built in both Anglo-Norman and Welsh areas, probably due to increased prosperity. It is interesting to speculate whether at this point in time there was a spate of yew planting in the associated churchyards.

Another potential indicator of the antiquity of a site is the existence of a holy well or spring. John Rhys, Professor of Celtic Studies at Oxford at the turn of the twentieth century, wrote an important paper in 1901 entitled 'The Pagan Folklore of Welsh Wells'. In the study he includes evidence of Welsh instances of the habit of tying rags to the branches of trees growing near a holy well. This ancient custom, found in many cultures and common to all Celtic regions, is connected with the riddance of illness and ailments through the 'offering' of the rag to the gods/God, or a local saint. In Rhys' words, 'the rag was regarded as the vehicle of a disease of which the ailing visitor to the well wished to be rid.' The further ritual of depositing a bead, button or coin (still common) in the water of the well formed an additional offering. They were later used to accompany prayers and wishes (hence the term Wishing Well).

Of the examples given by Rhys from various areas of Wales, *Ffynnon Cae Moch*, between Coychurch (*Llangrallo*) and Bridgend (*Pen-y-bont ar Ogwr*) had above it a thorn tree which had either been planted or grown wild and replaced an earlier thorn that had died. Rhys observed the hanging rags in 1892.

At *Ffynnon Marcross*, the interpretation by Dafydd Morganwg in *The History of Glamorgan* was that the custom of tying shreds of linen or cotton to the branches of a tree standing close by the well was an indication of healing. In north Wales, at *Ffynnon Eilian* at Llandrillo-yn-Rhos, the rags tied to nearby bushes were carefully secured by using woollen twine. In Wales and England the custom seems largely to have died out during the twentieth century, but still persists in isolated places in Ireland, Scotland and Cornwall.

What appeared to happen was that random trees took on a special 'venerated' state and so became an integral part of the whole holy well site. The practices associated with these wells had become assimilated into the Celtic Christian culture, despite the failed efforts to eliminate the practice by distant church authorities.

Over fifty years later, in 1953, Francis Jones in his well-researched book *The Holy Wells of Wales* (reprinted 1998) also investigated the pagan origins of wells and their adoption by early Christians. Jones gave examples of approximately 200 wells associated with ecclesiastical sites, many of which were dedicated to Celtic saints. The well may not necessarily be found within the confines of the churchyard (eg. Llanerfyl, Penegoes). These fast-disappearing early features have not received much in the way of archaeological investigation apart from some minor projects. Francis Jones gathered his information by personal correspondence and did not visit many of the sites featured in the study, so some caution is required on the information contained in the publication.

Included in Jones' list are well sites with associated yew trees. Listed are *Ffynnon Bedr* in Caernarfonshire, *Ffynnon Elias* in Llansanffraid Deuddwr, and a well at Abermule (*Abermiwl*), both in Montgomeryshire (*Maldwyn*). From Carmarthenshire (*Sir Gaerfyrddin*) the *Ffynnon Gwenlais* yew, which grows above the source of the Gwenlais stream and was mentioned by both Lhuyd in the late seventeenth century (who described a chapel, *Capel Gwenlais*, on the site), and Fenton in his 1804 tour of Wales. Jones also listed eight yews growing in a field near the Oxwich well and church (a yew grows above St Illtyd's Well in Oxwich churchyard today) and the St Fagan's Well and yew in south Wales, referred to by Richard Symonds in 1645. To repeat, the existence or record of a holy well associated with a saint is an additional indicator for identifying early medieval churchyards.

Although not one feature alone is conclusive, by gathering together a combination of saint's dedication, shape and size of *llan*, any in situ inscribed stones, shrines, relics, secondary relics (eg. hand bells), legends, 'Lives', plus associated wells or springs, a picture of the early medieval ecclesiastical landscape of Wales begins to take shape. Until more detailed excavation work has taken place across a range of sites the above criteria are what we have to go on. It can be said with certainty, though, that church sites existed at local level in Wales by at least the seventh or eighth century.

Chapter Five

Detailed studies of ancient yews and sites

The sites covered are Defynnog (SN92542793) in Breconshire, Gwytherin (SH87676147) and Llangernyw (SH87526744) in Conwy, Llanerfyl (SJ03400977) and Pennant Melangell (SJ02422654) in Montgomeryshire. By coincidence three of the five have churches dedicated to female saints. The sites have received varying degrees of historical and archaeological research in recent years. As to be expected ancient yews grow on all five.

Defynnog

Defynnog is a small settlement just east of the Afon Senni, south of Sennybridge (*Pont Senni*) and west of the old county town of Brecon (*Aberhonddu*). The village has lovely views south to the Brecon Beacons. The church, which occupies a prominent position next to two main north–south roads that meet at Defynnog after crossing the mountains, is also only a short distance from the road that links east and west Wales (now the A40). Defynnog's position near these age-old routes indicates that the church and churchyard held an important position on the northern edge of the Brecon Beacons in the early Christian period.

This *clas* site is dedicated to St Cynog who, we are told, was the illegitimate son of Brychan (AD 490-550) and a chieftain's daughter named Banhadlwedd (broom blossom/'the golden-haired one'). Brychan was of royal descent, being the son of an Irish prince. There are many legends surrounding St Cynog. By tradition he was baptised in Brecon and he was given a precious bracelet/torque by his father Brychan (of Brecon) as a sign of his royal descent. The torque was described in the twelfth century by *Giraldus Cambrensis* (Gerald of Wales) who wrote: 'I must not be silent concerning the collar that they call St Canuac's, for it is most like to gold in weight, nature and colour. It is in four pieces wrought round, joined together artificially and clefted in the middle, with a dog's head, the teeth projecting'. The elders of Brecon, however, refused to recognise Cynog as an heir to their kingdom, for although it was claimed that he was the eldest of Brychan's sons, he was illegitimate and therefore had no royal claim. In 1702 Hugh Thomas wrote 'Cynog retired from his father's court to a hermitage not far from the high road between Brecon and Battle and he became a 'holy man' without royal status, travelling up and down in a poor miserable habit and with a heavy ring of iron twisted together like a torque or wreath and which he wore around his head. He was the subject of scorn and derision and was nicknamed *Kynog Camarch* – the despised king'.

Cynog's *Gŵyl Mabsant* was commemorated at the time of his *Ffair a Bwla*. It was held in Defynnog on the second Thursday in October, and at this fair purchases were made for his wake on the following Sunday. The wake, with feasting and celebrations took place in front of the Bull Inn and lasted for a week. This custom continued until 1835, when it was replaced by a goose fair with a ritual enactment of 'carrying Cynog' taking place on the Monday, when a local volunteer dressed in a suit of old clothes and was carried in procession through the village before being thrown into the river to 'enhance' his dishevelled appearance so reminiscent of the saint. The 'actor' was then laughed at and ridiculed by the drunken revellers.

The use of the Defynnog site in the fifth or sixth century is confirmed by the existence of the 'Stone of Rugniatis' found here and now positioned in the outer church porch. This pillar stone displays faint traces of old Irish ogham script and Latin memorial lettering that reads *'Rugniatio Livenoni'*. In the seventh to ninth centuries a double-headed Celtic ring cross was added to the early inscriptions. On the east wall of the porch is a pre-Norman holy water stoup and inside the church is a unique eleventh-century font with both 'Viking' Runic script and Lombardic writing. The main body of the church building dates from the fifteenth century but earlier traces exist on the northern side. The huge churchyard, the second largest in Breconshire, has almost certainly been extended out from its original *llan* enclosure. Within or on the first boundary banks are no fewer than four ancient female yews. On the south-east side of the church entrance porch the huge bole of a low-growing yew slowly breaks free from its surrounding wall. This old giant of a tree, measuring well over 8 metres round, was host in 2006 to a colony of Norway wasps whose beautiful nest hung below a low bough just above a path!

To the west a tall columnar conifer grows on mounded ground, perhaps once the home of a long departed 'fifth' ancient yew? On the north-east side of the church an unusually tall old yew is looked over by a row of cottages whose windows are at eye level with the banked grassy churchyard. The girth of this yew measures slightly less than 8 metres.

The real treat at Defynnog for the yew enthusiast is to be found not far away on the northern side of the church building. Here some 20 metres from the church two female yews grow within 6 metres of each other. When viewed from the church tower their crowns appear as one great spreading mass of green, but at ground level a table tomb from AD 1800 sits in deep shade between the two trees. Of the two yews the larger is the easterly one (furthest away from the tower) measuring in excess of 11 metres. Only when ducking below the spreading branches can the enormity of the base be observed. Here a tangle of over seven secondary limbs emanate from the slowly rotting core. Each of these limbs is itself worthy of the status of a tree. The other female yew, although impressive and old, does not have the extremely aged appearance of its neighbour. It measures just short of 7 metres. It has been suggested that these two female trees may grow from the same root system, as both have a similar growth style and both suffer from the common yew condition of browning of the shoots (branchlets) of the previous year's growth (2008). If they are layered they would constitute the biggest (over 20 metres round existing parts) and probably the oldest of any existing yew trees in Europe. It is more likely that the bigger of the two trees is the parent of the other.

Only excavation or DNA testing can confirm whether this is the case (see p. 97). The yews have all had walls built around them, probably in the eighteenth century. These are now slowly crumbling away as the boles of the trees increase outwards.

The combination of an early inscribed stone, a saint and his recorded legend, and some of the most impressive yews in Wales make Defynnog one of the most important and thought-provoking places to visit.

Gwytherin

Gwytherin is a small and remote village on the Denbighshire moors, with a church dedicated to St Gwenfrewi (Winifred). The church building stands at the highest point of the churchyard, on a promontory, and the site is classified as early medieval. Interestingly it may once have held a double monastery. On the north side the ground falls steeply away down to a stream that forms the northern boundary of the present enclosure. To the south and east sides the land falls less steeply and the boundary on those sides is now at the foot of the slope. The present church was re-built in 1867-9 and like its predecessor consists of a single chamber. The north wall is a remnant of an earlier fourteenth-century church, and set in the sanctuary step is a decorative cross slab of a similar date. According to tradition the original church was founded by St Eleri. When it was rebuilt at some early unknown date it was re-dedicated to St James, before it became dilapidated again and rebuilt after 1869.

On the land to the south of the churchyard once stood the chapel of Gwenfrewi. In 1698 Edward Lhuyd produced a drawing captioned 'A Tombstone at Kappel Gwenfrewi in ye south part of Gwetherin Churchyard'. In 1710 the Rural Dean, Thomas Williams reported that there remained a 'little ruined chapell' and in 1729 there was a further report that it had been 'converted into a dwelling house for a poor widow to live in and she also made use of the yard for a garden'. Thomas Pennant wrote in 1784 that *Capel Gwenfrewi* (also known later as Penbryn Chapel) was totally destroyed and nothing remained except the outline of ditches and chapel foundations. Recent investigations show that in the centre of the small field is a flat-topped hillock on which there is a shallow depression 3 metres in diameter. All evidence suggests this is site of the early chapel. It is assumed that the stone built chapel observed by Lhuyd replaced the wooden '*ecclesiola*' or '*capel y beddau*' referred to by Robert of Shrewsbury in the early twelfth century. Robert's *Translatio* tells us that the original wooden chapel was always kept open and the shrine consisted of a slab carved with a representation of St Winifred. Shrine chapels are not an uncommon feature of early medieval Wales. They also existed in Ireland, and Robert's description is similar to surviving shrine slabs on Anglesey and in Brittany. These shrines sometimes held empty graves.

Of great interest in the Rural Dean's report of 1710 is the mention of an old reliquary held in the church and supposedly holding the remains of, or the probable secondary relics of, St Gwenfrewi. Two fragments of the oak reliquary, illustrated by Lhuyd in 1698 and known as *Arch Gwenfrewi*, turned up unexpectedly in the late twentieth century. Lhuyd's drawing shows one gable end and the adjoining face of a triangular shrine. The depicted decoration has been described as having similarities with Anglo-Saxon ornamental metalwork of the eighth or early ninth century, although it may have been made in Wales. The above information proves that Christian activity at Gwytherin can be dated to at least the early ninth century. Apart from a recently discovered fragment at Llangorse Crannog in Breconshire, it is unique to find such an example of a tent-shaped shrine in Wales. The similarities with St Manchan's reliquary in Ireland adds weight to the Irish influence on the Gwytherin area during the early medieval period.

The entire curvilinear site at Gwytherin, including the present churchyard and the small field, has similarities to other large *llannau* in Wales (eg. Defynnog, Llanafan Fawr). These big enclosures are regarded as monastic sites dating from the early medieval period. This site, however, is unique in Wales as nowhere else is there to be found what appears to be a *llan* within a *llan*. Aerial photographs and maps confirm the line of a clear boundary around both enclosures forming a large and distinct oval shape.

The four standing stones located between the stream and the north side of the church at Gwytherin have prompted much discussion over the years. In 1710 there was mention of only two standing stones, so between then and 1784 when four stones were reported, two further stones were added. They may have been put there to act as a barrier to the steep drop down to the stream. It is possible they were resited from the lower saints' graveyard, that which had contained *Capel Gwenfrewi*. By the early nineteenth century the line of stones was being shown on maps as the site of Gwenfrewi's grave. The most westerly or 'Vinnemaglus' stone bears the Latin inscription 'Vinnemagli Fili Senemagli'. The formula 'son of' and the names themselves add to the impression that Gwytherin was part of an Irish settlement in the early medieval period. Nash-Williams dated the Latin inscription to the late fifth or early sixth century.

Regarding the legend of St Gwenfrewi, the principal sources for her 'Life' are the anonymous *Vita Prima* composed before 1138, probably by a monk of St Werburgh's Abbey in Chester, and the *Vita Secunda*. This second and more important work dated shortly after the removal of the relics of St Gwenfrewi from Holywell to Shrewsbury in 1138, is attributed to Robert, Prior of the Benedictine Abbey of Shrewsbury. He is seen as the principal influence for the moving of the relics, probably for political purposes. According to Hulse, the *Vita Secunda* portrays a clear picture of the Gwytherin *llan* as the centre of a saint's cult in the twelfth century. However the dating of the reliquary demonstrates Gwenfrewi was venerated at Gwytherin 400 years before Robert wrote his *Vita Secunda*. Hulse argues strongly for the authenticity of much of Robert's *Vita*.

There is much detail in Robert's work, including Gwenfrewi's death date of 2 November, and her request to be buried beside her former abbess Tenoi at Gwytherin. Other saints lay nearby, but it was Gwenfrewi's grave that became a source of cures and wonders and therefore a place of pilgrimage. Abbot Eleri, Gwenfrewi's confessor, was buried in the church bearing his name, where his relics were supposed to work miracles. Robert gives a good description of the saints' graveyard, fenced off from the higher cemetery on which stood the small wooden chapel referred to as the 'ecclesiola' (little church). Robert also describes an 'ancient oak' growing amongst the graves 'out of veneration for the buried saints'. Miracles regarding this 'sacred tree' and its protective powers give an added dimension to the inviolability of the saints' *llan*. Here in twelfth-century Wales is written recognition of a special tree associated with the graveyard of a saint. Although not a yew it gives authority to the role a tree could play on a religious site in the Celtic west. This role, akin to the pagan 'kingship' tree, the Irish '*Bile*' and saints' trees of Ireland, shows the legacy of the pre-Christian still existed in the medieval period.

In the present churchyard grow three large female yews, an undetermined fourth, and a much younger yew. The female tree located on the easterly side of the present church, 8 metres away from the chancel, has a large hollow portion of trunk on its northerly side. This hollow stem is recovering from extensive fire damage that occured during the 1980s. Low down, the main bole splits into two, below that point the girth measures over 8.5 metres. The other impressively-sized female tree is located approximately 8 metres to the west of the church. This yew is hollow and is almost identical in girth to the westerly female, but less branched. However, the crown of the tree spreads out over 12 metres. Both these female trees are within the top fifty largest yews in Wales. The third female tree grows to the south west of the present church structure and overhangs the churchyard path. This is also a wide-spreading tree but its appearance and girth (just below 6 metres) leads one to believe it is considerably younger than the other two. The fourth tree, growing on the steep north-eastern bank, is probably an offspring from one of the older yews. No trees of any species grow in the 'chapel field'.

There appear to be no known historic records relating to the churchyard yews. The positioning of the two biggest yews, 8 metres either side of the present church, gives the disinct impression that their planting, at whatever period, was related to the earliest structure built at the centre of that mound. The fourteenth-century inscribed medieval slab is the earliest surviving church evidence, but the pre-Norman *Capel Gwenfrewi*, and possibly the reliquary, relate to the chapel field and not the church mound. Questions remain, therefore. Was there an early medieval church at the same time as the *capel*? If not, was the first church built post-Conquest? If the latter is the case, the oldest yews are likely to be only medieval trees.

The other question relates to the role and position of the standing stones, argued by many as being not only proof of the pagan origins of the mound, but also that they are in some way associated to the age of the yews (meaning thousands of years old). Were they moved from elsewhere to the church mound at some date later than the ninth century? Further research is required to get closer to answering these questions. Robert of Shrewsbury did not mention yew trees in his text, only the sacred oak, so did they exist at the time he wrote the 'Life'? Whatever the answer it must be remembered that a textual omission does not automatically indicate that they did not grow at Gwytherin at that time.

Llangernyw

Llangernyw is a small settlement in a remote part of the eastern Conwy valley hills. The village lies south-west of Abergele on the A548, a road that follows the old drovers' route from Llanrwst. To the south-east down a narrow valley is Gwytherin, featured previously. The church at Llangernyw comes under the care of the diocese of St Asaph and is dedicated to St Digain, whose feast day is 21 November. The church is built in a cruciform shape, which is unusual in this part of north Wales. Fairly recently an extensive restoration programme has taken place, included the whitewashing of the church walls, a project undertaken under the direction of CADW.

The foundation of the site is without doubt early medieval, confirmed by the existence of two early inscribed pillar stones sited to the south of the church and dating from between the seventh to ninth centuries. These are positioned close to a pair of uncut boulders that stand either side of a raised grave slab. These boulders give credence to the view that the site was used in pre-Christian times for some form of ritual religious behaviour, as yet undetermined. Whether all these stones are in their original positions is unknown, but if not we must still assume they were located somewhere in the churchyard enclosure. The present churchyard is now an elongated 'lozenge' shape but the heart of the *llan* is curvilinear. To the south the ground falls very sharply away to a valley. To the south-east corner a curved scarp may have formed an original boundary bank.

Folk history informs us that the church was founded by the fifth-century St Digain, the son of *Cystenyn Gorneu* (Gernyw), (Constantine the Blessed of Cornwall). Llangernyw is the only church in Wales dedicated to Digain. (The similar-sounding Llangynyw in Mongomeryshire has a Cynyw dedication.) Although none of the present church building dates from prior to the thirteenth century there must have been some form of structure here in pre-Norman times, of which there is now no trace. A further indication of early Christian activity is the holy well of *Ffynnon Digain* (SH87146833) located a little way to the north side of the village. Additions and alterations have taken place to St Digain's church over the past seven centuries right up till the Victorian period.

Dominating the northern side of the church, when entering through the lych gate, is the enormous wide-spreading, male yew tree. It is split into four main fragments, with the most southerly piece bending low to touch the ground. Measuring around the surviving pieces a reading of 10 metres is easily achieved. Until the 1990s, a large oil tank was positioned in the centre of the tree. It is possible that this tank exaggerated the spreading nature of the branches. After the yew had received national fame on account of its size, the oil tank was removed and the whole area around the base of the tree was tidied up – perhaps a little too much, as valuable bits of old growth have been removed. Nevertheless the removal of the tank and recognition of the antiquity of the tree have been of positive benefit to its long-term future. The Llangernyw yew is often described as exceeding 4,000 years old, and thus was identified as one of the *50 Great British Trees* by the Tree Council, which has given it both national and international status. The extreme age assessment originated from Allan Meredith's Gazetteer of 1996. It is legitimate to claim the tree as one of the oldest and most impressive yews in Wales, with a history at least back to the inscribed stones. Whether it was growing before the easliest saint set up his oratory here in the fifth or sixth century, we cannot say.

Llanerfyl

The small settlement of Llanerfyl lies on relatively high ground on the ancient route that crosses central Wales east to west, once linking Roman *Viriconium* to Caernarfon. Not far away from Llanerfyl is the route of the old Roman north to south road that dissected Wales passing through what is now known as the Cann Office near Llangadfan. It is no coincidence that in the late Roman–early Christian period, the churchyard at Llanerfyl was, like Defynnog, strategically positioned close to two major Roman routes.

Llanerfyl's mounded churchyard is roughly circular and sits high above the river Banwy, which flows to its west and north. The parish church is dedicated to St Erfyl, by tradition a sixth-century virgin saint. The enclosure is clearly of some antiquity, endorsed by other key features found at the site, namely an early inscribed memorial stone, a shrine and a reliquary. The stone is now sited within the church and has been described as either 'the last inscription of Roman Britain or the first early medieval inscription of Wales'. The stone commemorates a thirteen-year-old girl named Rosteece (or Rostece).

The inscription reads:

HIC [IN]
TVM[V]LOIA
CIT.R[O]STE
CE.FILIA.PA
TERNINI.
ANIXIII.IN
PA (ce)

Translated it reads: 'Here in the tomb lies Rosteece, daughter of Paterninus, aged 13. In peace'. It has been identified as a Christian memorial and has been dated between the mid fifth and early sixth centuries. The inscribed stone was formerly sited under the big old yew tree and was first recorded in 1791.

On a wall inside the church is an undated account by Archdeacon Thomas describing the circumstances that resulted in the moving of the stone in the summer of 1915. The account recalls damage to the big yew during the winter of 1914-5 when one of the great 'arms' was broken by the force and weight of a violent snow storm. Happily it was on the opposite side to the stone: '... had it been its own overshadowing arm, it must have inflicted serious perhaps irreparable damage to it.' Consequently, the rector, Rev T. D. James, who gave the Archdeacon the details for the article, decided after consultation to have the stone removed into the church for its better preservation. This was done on 6th July 1915. The stone now stands upright against the west wall facing the nave, where it can be 'more readily scanned by the curious and the student, and tell its message of Peace to future generations. A marked boulder points out its old position beneath the spreading yew tree'. This account is contradicted by Jeremy Knight, who writes that the stone was moved into the church during the nineteenth century, and not the twentieth, as described by Archdeacon Thomas. We cannot say whether the position of the inscribed stone under the yew was the original or intended site, but it is not surprising that the memorial stone has long been connected in legend with the patron saint Erfyl.

Located to the left of the altar and standing at just over 2 metres tall and 80 centimetres wide is a rare oak shrine. It is believed to date from the fifteenth century and probably held a statue of St Erfyl. It was a general rule from the fourteenth century onwards that a depiction of the patron saint be displayed in the chancel of parish churches. To the right of the altar is the oak reliquary, originally sited on top of the shrine but believed to predate it. It measures approximately 70 centimetres high and wide, and is 25 centimetres deep. It would have been carried on staves in the patronal feast procession. The true purpose of the reliquary was to contain a precious casket of silver, ivory or crystal, in which the saint's bones or secondary relics were enshrined. Another indication of the antiquity of the site is the record of St Erfyl's well, located approximately 400 metres to the north-west of the church, and still in use until midway through the twentieth century for the supply of baptismal water.

Llanerfyl most probably played an important role as a centre of early Christianity after the Roman occupation of the region. As already mentioned, Llanerfyl is on an ancient main route from Wroxeter (Roman *Viriconium*) and within the old tribal territory of the *Cornovii*. To date, Wroxeter has produced a fifth-century memorial stone, and the possibility of a Roman Church on the site has not been entirely discounted. The other close major route linked the south to the Roman military strongholds of the north, and during the Roman period the principal military stations *Segontium* (Caernarfon), Brecon and Llanio (Ceredigion) had roads connecting these centres. The stations would have attracted particular attention in the period of the Christian advancement over the Roman population. These military stations were evacuated by 400 AD and Britain became severed from the main Roman Empire by 410-415 AD.

The Llanerfyl churchyard yew, known locally as 'the Patriarch' even though most of the growth is female, is considered to be one of the oldest churchyard yews in Wales. It has probably gained this distinction due in part to the vast area covered by its crown and its broken and fragmented limbs, which conveys a feeling of extreme antiquity. One of the latest reports on the tree was carried out in 1999 (CPAT) and reads as follows: 'The yew is split into four trunks and its branches have curled and spread out widely. A low stone revetment wall encircles the yew; a stone pillar supports its western trunk and a wooden prop supports the east side.'

The following poem by D. James (1901-1927) is displayed within the church:

Un bonyn ywen bena-byw ydyw,	The one main yew tree stem still lives,
Yn bedwar gwasgara,	Spreading outward into four,
Fel pedwar pren, cliben da,	As 'twere four trees with good intent
Yn gyd fawr hardd gysgodfa.	Give shelter far and wide.
Y tramawr gangau trymion-bywcad,	The great and massive branches
A bwysant ar bolion,	Lean on supporting poles,
Breuawl, diffygiawl heb fforc,	Brittle and failing, if unpropped,
Aeth harddwch y bythwyrddion.	Gone is the beauty of the evergreens.

The ancient yew grows to the south of the church directly in front of the porch. In fact the yew's huge bulk dominates that area of the churchyard. Previous tree reports mention four or five main stems, but I would suggest there are only three. Detailed observation shows that the three stems to the rear of the tree (as viewed from the porch) are all connected. One 'piece' has fallen through a rotted trunk and is now supported by a brick pillar (after 1915). The easterly limb, which is very twisted (probably caused by the storm damage of 1915), is now propped up by wooden 'supports', which incidentally are of little use in the present circumstances. This easterly limb exceeds 4 metres in girth. The north-westerly limb, almost completely rotted away but not quite, has layered into the ground near the path. That limb is male, the rest of the yew is female. The male limb spreads across to the east and grows into the rest of the crown so making identification of the different parts of the tree difficult without close scrutiny. The low wall is undated but reference to other 'yew walls' in Wales show them to be mainly eighteenth-century creations.This wall though was probably rebuilt after the storm damage of 1915.

It is difficult to imagine the tree in its original state before it started breaking up. The male limb poses some questions about its origin, but I would strongly suggest that it is at one with the rest of the tree, that is it comes out of the same rootstock. The base of the male limb seems to eminate from a central core point of the original growth. Only DNA testing can definitely confirm this opinion. Until such time as that testing is carried out all the growth should be treated as the one tree. The spread of the whole yew covers more than 30 metres. Although it cannot be proven that the yew was planted as a saint's tree at the early establishment of Christianity at Llanerfyl, the occurrence of the *Rosteece* stone together with one of the biggest yews in Wales seems more than coincidence. However, one site alone cannot provide all the answers. Other such occurrences of early churchyard features and the biggest yews provide a pattern, and therefore a more compelling argument as to the yews' age and their reasons for growing on those sites.

Pennant Melangell

The settlement of Pennant Melangell is found near the head of the Tanat valley in west Montgomeryshire. Its remote location indicates that it may once have functioned as a hermitage site. The church at Pennant is dedicated to the female saint Melangell (*Monacella*). Under the Normans it was dedicated to St Michael, with the place name Llanfihangel-y-Pennant existing on maps until at least the eighteenth century. However enough evidence exists to associate the site with Melangell. Her 'Life', *Historia divae Monacellae*, survives in two variants, both of a post-Reformation date, although they are both believed to originate out of late medieval source material. The Welsh Genealogies imply that the saint was born in the late sixth century, in the same period as that suggested by the *Historia*. Interestingly the 'Life' talks of both a female community founded by Melangell, and a male community of abbots living under Melangell's sanctuary (*liberi tenentes dict' abbates tui sanctuarii*). Like Gwytherin, Pennant appeared to have had a double community sharing the same site.

The relatively large, curvilinear churchyard at Pennant measures 80 metres across north to south, and 95 metres east to west. It covers just over half of a hectare, and over 1000 burials have been recorded at Pennant since burial records began, of which the great majority are unmarked. The earliest burial record is from 1680. It is estimated that somewhere between 1000 and 2000 burials have taken place since the twelfth century. In the later medieval period Pennant probably became the final resting place of former pilgrims from beyond the parish. The late fifteenth-century elegy to Einion ap Gruffudd of Llechwedd Ysrad (d.1493) bears witness to this. It is noted that at Pennant some form of continuity or re-use of a pre-existing pagan burial ground took place. Churches such as St Melangell's at Pennant Melangell may have started life simply as enclosed cemeteries, to which a church only became established as late as perhaps the eleventh or twelfth centuries. Other associations between Bronze Age burial sites and early Christian enclosures suggest that there may have been a Bronze Age burial mound at Pennant, possibly below the present church. It may be that the earlier pagan site was used in later times either because it was already 'sanctified' in some way, or because the presence of an existing place of veneration gave the local community 'authorisation' to continue its use as a place of burial. The earlier cemetery appears to have continued in use until just before the stone church was constructed in the twelfth century. The archaeological work carried out in the 1980s and 1990s by CPAT, and reported in *Montgomeryshire Collections 82*, revealed small quantities of cremated bone located in some small charcoal filled pits. The contents of some of the pits represent the disposal of cremation pyres from the Bronze Age, so proving that the site was in use in the pre-Christian period. Charred plant remains taken from Pennant Melangell during the archaeological work show that of the various tree species found, including oak, alder, elm and beech, there was no yew found.

There are now seven yews growing in the churchyard, one of them recently planted. The yew tree to the north of the church was planted in the spring of 1878 to commemorate the church restoration work of 1876-7. Four of the other six yews are of considerable age with trunk diameters measuring up to 3.5 metres across; two of these trees, one male and one female, both growing on the eastern perimeter bank of the churchyard, look to be the oldest. The male tree to the east of the Apse has a girth exceeding 8.5 metres. The female yew next to the lych gate is over 7 metres in girth. Another male tree on the southerly boundary has what is fairly uncommon for a churchyard yew: a layering branch. The big spreading female yew to the west grows well within the boundary of the present churchyard. A number of the yews are set on mounds up to a metre high, which are probably comprised of earth and stone disposed of during grave digging. This feature is not an uncommon site in old churchyards. The appearance at Pennant of a low mound, approximately 25 metres to the north-west of the church, may have been where a further yew once grew. The position of the 'restoration' yew to the north of the church corresponds fairly closely with the recorded site of a cockpit.

Appearing under 'Items of Expenditure' in the parish accounts during the early and mid eighteenth century are the following notes concerning walling work. The first reference is from 1715: 'for making a new wall about two of the yew trees toward their maintenance to grow' and an entry in 1757 reads: 'walling about the yew trees'. The trees would have been of considerable size at the time of walling, so indicating at least a medieval origin. The building of the walls 'towards their maintenance to grow' as described in the Pennant Parish Vestry Accounts and Minutes of 1712 to 1840, gives a valuable indication of the importance the yews in the *llan*.

In 1894 when the Reverend Elias Owen of Llanyblodwel was conducting a tour of Pennant for the Cambrian Society he referred to the 'magnificent yews'. He pointed to the 'still visible marks of the lopping they underwent in Plantagenet times (Henry II–Richard III) when the men were required to exercise themselves in archery on Sunday afternoons and when they naturally resorted to the yew trees for bows'. Whether this observation was correct or merely a 'flight of fancy' we cannot say, but it seems far-fetched.

Pennant has the remains of a Romanesque shrine and an early foundation date, possibly about the eighth century, associated with the legend of Melangell. Although poorly dated and historically unreliable, the legend is important for the questions it raises about the early structure of the Christian church in the Tanat valley. The apse and Romanesque shrine are evidence of the twelfth-century cult devoted to the local female saint. However, because of the hidden nature of the site the cult could have existed long before that time. Other finds from Pennant include a fragmentary red glass bead of an Anglo-Saxon style recovered from a ditch, probably of a sixth- or seventh-century date.

The apse and arched opening at the eastern end of the existing church were purposely constructed to enclose a stone-edged grave that by tradition held the remains of Melangell. It is probable that this grave pre-dates the twelfth-century church. St Melangell is portrayed as an abbess on the rood screen in Pennant Melangell, and Thomas Sebastian Price, a local scholar from Llanfyllin, writing in the seventeenth century, recorded the custom of protecting St Monacella's hares in the parish. Thomas Pennant (1726-98), visiting the parish in the eighteenth century, noted that devotion to the patroness of hares still continued. Melangell's association with hares represents the assimilation of pagan beliefs about the sacred character of the hare into the Christian period. It is not known for certain whether she was given land by a King Brochwel as described, or whether she did actually exist. However, the best way to explain her cult, as with that of other Welsh saints, is to accept that at some point in history she did live in the Pennant valley.

Further evidence of the importance of the Pennant area is found in the name of the nearby farm of *Tyn-y-cablyd*, near the source of the Afon Tanat at the head of Cwm Pennant. The farm takes its name from *Dydd Iau Cablyd*, translated as Maundy Thursday, traditionally the day upon which those of high church rank washed the feet of, and gave gifts to, the poor. The name adds to the impression that this whole end of the cwm, incorporating the *llan*, was part of a larger sacred landscape.

The great interest at Pennant is the recent archaeological work and its findings. The reference to the maintenance of the yew trees is also of great historical value. The proven pre-Christian usage of the site tempts us to link the age of the yews with that early period, but the trees may have been planted to delineate the Christian boundary of the site.

Travelogue

100 of the best yew tree sites in Wales region by region

From the early days of Christianity in Wales, successive generations cared for and maintained their churchyard yews, sometimes putting a monetary value on the tree to protect it. In the eighteenth century, walls were built around them and the Victorians added iron bands, props and cables. Some of these practices may now be seen as somewhat misguided, but the attitude of concern must be applauded: these great *living* monuments deserve our attention.

Care must be taken to avoid any potential damage to the trees, the surrounding ground and indeed to the whole site. We too must respect these great old yews and allow them to continue to live as part of the churchyard scene for many more years to come.

Snowdonia and north-western Wales

While Anglesey and the Llŷn Peninsula are rich in the early Christian history of Wales, they lack significant yews. The dominant landmass of Snowdonia is a natural curtailer of likely sites. However what the region lacks in yew numbers it makes up for not only in worthwhile sites, but in inspiring landscapes.

Caerhun (SH 77687040)

Many yews

We start our journey at Caerhun on the west side of the Afon Conwy. The village is situated on the B5106, and the church of St Mary is in a prominent position overlooking the river and is found down a minor track indicated by a small finger-sign.

The churchyard sits in the north-east corner of Roman *Canovium*, an auxiliary fort administered from *Deva* (Chester). *Canovium* occupied not only a good defensive position but was a key strategic site for the control of this area of north-west Wales. The oldest parts of St Mary's church are thought to date back to the thirteenth century, but it is perfectly possible that an earlier Christian settlement preceded it. The signs of the Roman occupation are still to be seen on the south and south-eastern corner of the churchyard where the Roman ramparts remain. An impressive ring of dark green yews surround the church and stand out starkly against it and the surrounding landscape. John Lowe, the yew tree recorder, referred to the Caerhun yews in his 1897 publication *The Yew Trees of Britain and Ireland*. The trees are all female apart from one male on the south-western side, which is the second largest measuring over 6 metres. The yews provide valuable shelter in this exposed but beautiful churchyard.

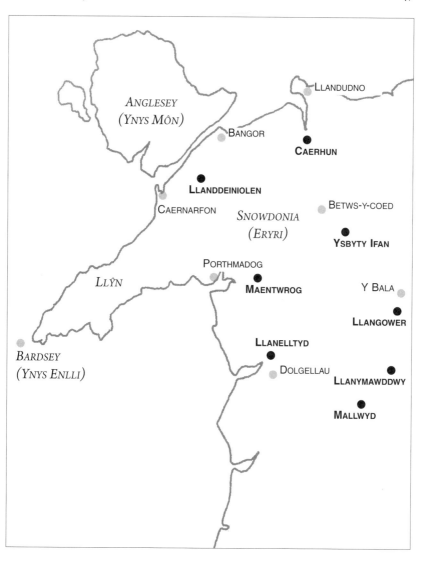

Snowdonia and north-western Wales

Close to Caerhun on the opposite side of the B5106, a lane at Tal-y-bont leads up to the small village of Llanbedr-y-cennin. On the left-hand side of the lane is a marked footpath to the property *Ffynnon Bedr* (St Peter's well). From this footpath and viewed across the field to the right (now on private land) is the holy well from which the dwelling gets its name. The well is now dry but it was documented in 1954 by Francis Jones in his excellent reference book *The Holy Wells of Wales*. The well had at one time been a place of pilgrimage and had a small building above it, and up to the Victorian period sick children were bathed there and afterwards taken to a small chapel nearby. The well building no longer stands, but the 7-metre female yew growing above the well and described by Francis Jones does still stand, albeit in a declining state. It is of some considerable age and must have been planted in at least the middle ages to endorse the holy or sacred aspect of this place.

Llanddeiniolen (SH 54576593)

Three old yews

Amongst the largest and oldest yews to be found in Snowdonia are those growing in the churchyard of St Deiniolen at Llanddeiniolen. The church and churchyard are situated just to the south of the B4366 inland from Bangor. As long ago as 1834 the yews were recorded, and of the three 'ancients' the biggest marginally is a male tree measuring well over 8 metres. All three yews are of a similar age with one being unmeasurable, for a low horizontal fork impedes accurate 'taping'. There is no site in Wales where the yews give such a powerful, gloomy presence than at Llanddeiniolen. The well dedicated to Deiniolen (*Ffynnon Deiniolen*) was located some way south of the church further down the lane.

Maentwrog (SH 66454053)

Three old yews

In the vale of Ffestiniog a short distance from Harlech and Porthmadog and the old Roman road *Sarn Helen*, where the old bridge crosses the Afon Dwyryd just south of the A487, is the village of Maentwrog. The place-name translates as 'the stone of Twrog', a Celtic man who was either a mythical giant or more likely an early saint. He is also dedicated at Llandwrog south of Caernarfon. Twrog's stone is a 4-foot sandstone pillar, which stands next to the west end of the church. Of the several big old yews adorning the churchyard the largest is a female tree to the south, measuring almost 7 metres round.

Llanelltyd (SH 71751954)

Two old yews

North-west of Dolgellau on the north side of the Mawddach is the settlement Llanelltyd, which has a small unpretentious church dedicated to that most famous of early saints, Illtyd, the only such dedication in north Wales. The first mention of St Illtyd (Elltud, IItut) is from the 'Life' of St Samson in AD 610: Illtyd was credited with being 'the most learned of the Britons in knowledge and scripture'. His celebrated

The fluted trunk of the Carno yew, Mid Wales

Llantysilio – To the west of the redundant church grows a yew needing close inspection to reveal its age. Remains of the original trunk can be seen just above ground level (left foreground). There may be many 'remnant' yews similar to this, growing undetected in Welsh churchyards.

Llanedryn – a once great tree has had to endure extensive fire damage in recent years. It still though clings to life.

Old print of Betws Newydd yew showing internal stem (1874)

Betws Newydd yew today

Three of the four stems remain at Llandre

Llanfihangel Genau'r Glyn – 1874 drawing of the Llandre yew showing four stems

Llandrillo – now in two sections. The rebuilt wall now incorporates a fallen stem (right foreground).

Nineteenth-century depiction of Llandrillo. An exaggeratedly small figure stands next to the stunted tree. Note the small enclosing wall.

Defynnog – from above the two female yews look as one

One of the big Gwytherin yews. The hollow left bole still bears the scars of past fire damage.

*Early morning frost lies on the ground in front of
Llangernyw's ancient yew*

Llanerfyl – one of Wales' most remarkable yews

Pennant Melangell – one giant yew growing on a mound by the lych gate

The shrine of St Melangell

Caerhun – church and yews within the corner of a Roman fort above Afon Conwy

The huge old yews in the churchyard at Llanddeiniolen

*Llangower – the single immense female yew by the redundant church
near the shores of Llyn Tegid*

*Ysbyty Ifan – 'the pilgrim church of St John' is home
to three closely-growing female yews*

The stone steps and pulpit inside the hollow centre of the Nantglyn yew

The hollow walled yew in St Beuno's churchyard at Gwyddelwern

St Derfel's famous wooden horse/stag and his staff at Llandderfel

One of the remaining Llandderfel yews

Llangynyw (Powys) – the whitewashed church stands out starkly amidst the dark green, almost black, yews

Looking through the fragments of Overton's oldest yew to the iron railings beyond

Gresford – an early photograph of the railed ancient yew

Llandinam – an historic churchyard in the Vale of the Severn. The yew by tradition is eight hundred years old.

Llanbadarn-y-Garreg – the only church in Radnorshire dedicated to St Padarn. The leaning yew has an internal stem.

Llanafan Fawr – inscribed stones built into the porch wall tell of an early medieval past

The biggest of Llanspyddid's eight old yews

Llanspyddid – the 7th/8th C. inscribed stone known as 'The Cross of Brychan Brycheiniog'

The old yew at Llandybïe has a small cropped crown, but the bole gives away its age

Goetre – a classic position by the path and near the porch for this ancient yew

The 'old' church and yew at Penallt look out over the Wye Valley to the woods beyond

61

The graceful yew at St Brides-super-Ely overlooks the small church

Cil-y-cwm – the biggest yew has unusual light coloured bark. It stands in front of a whitewashed out-house near a gate which leads to the river bank.

Llanrhidian – the yew towers over the church and looks towards the sea and salt marshes

The deserted 'pilgrim' church of Llanfihangel Abercywyn with its yew seen through the ruins

St Dogmaels (Llandudoch) – the living parts of the yew are contained within a high wall.

The sun breaks through the dense shade created by the avenue of eight yews at Nevern. The 'bleeding' yew is second on the right from the gate.

Llanfihangel Ystrad Aeron – a relatively unknown but impressive giant in the Aeron valley

school was at Llantwit Major (*Llanilltyd Fawr*) in the Vale of Glamorgan in south-east Wales. Near Llanelltyd in 1199 the Cistercians founded the monastery at Cymer Abbey and from there they supplied priests to administer Llanelltyd church.

The present simple structure is approached from a path passing between two large Irish yews. The churchyard enclosure is both circular and raised and on a clear day gives good views of the spectacular mountain, Cader Idris, which rises up behind Dolgellau. There are several old yews on site but the female tree growing south (behind) the church and the low-branching male to the north are the oldest and of considerable age.

Within the church are items of local historical interest including, under the west window, an unusual inscribed stone bearing the imprint of a foot and dated from before the first recorded church here in the thirteenth century. Kenric's Stone was discovered in an outbuilding in 1876 and is so named for its inscription that tells us that a Kenric (Cynwrig), who was probably a pilgrim, set out from here to 'foreign parts' many centuries ago.

On the north wall of the church is an unusual script that attempts to explain why early churchyards are circular in shape. Reference is made to the right of fugitives to seek sanctuary within the 'holy circle' for up to seven years and seven days (see Llandrillo, p. 71). The circle was apparently defined from a central point by a ploughman and his plough team who travelled in a clockwise direction from the centre setting the outer boundary of the enclosure. This was later referred to as 'God's Acre', the holy 'protected' ground surrounding the church. The undated description is an intriguing mix of the fanciful and the true, rooted in both Celtic folklore and early Irish and Welsh legal tracts. St Illtyd's church can now be included in 'a tour' of some of north-west Wales's early church sites.

The whole area around Llanelltyd is noted for its vast scenic vistas and wonderful walking, the New Precipice Walk on the north side of the estuary being one of the best.

Mallwyd (SH 8628135)

Three old yews including one giant tree

South-east of Dolgellau and east of the Afon Dyfi there is a division of routes, south to Machynlleth and east to Welshpool. Here at Mallwyd, by the Brigands' Inn (named after the famous red haired bandits who once controlled this area), is the church of St Tydecho with its seventeenth-century plank tower and tiered gallery. Mounted somewhat bizarrely above the doorway is the vertebra of a prehistoric ox. The scholar John Davies, who achieved fame for his authorship of the Welsh-Latin dictionary, was once rector at Mallwyd.

In the churchyard are several very large yews. To the east of the church close to the wall is the biggest, a truly ancient male tree measuring over 10 metres, a specimen surely as old as the time when the Breton saint Tydecho established his *llan* here in the sixth century. In 1854 George Borrow visited the church on his tour of *Wild Wales* and described the male tree as follows: 'An immense yew tree grows in the churchyard and partly overshadows the road with its branches'. Fourteen years later, in Black's

Picturesque Guide to North and South Wales (1868), the biggest yew at Mallwyd was described as 'of extraordinary size and luxuriance' with a trunk of 'twenty two feet and six inches'.

Llanymawddwy (SH 90331904)

Five stems grow from old base of great yew

Another ancient yew noted in 1868 was the one growing in Llanymawddwy churchyard. This Meirionnydd site is situated in the remote upper Dyfi valley, north of Mallwyd and Dinas Mawddwy, below the Aran Fawddwy mountain ridge. The old drovers' road beyond Llanymawddwy goes up to the awesome *Bwlch y Groes* ('pass of the cross'), the highest pass in Wales, a route that seems almost as ancient as the mountains themselves. From there the road drops down to the south-eastern end of Llyn Tegid. Llanymawddwy catered for pilgrims, drovers and any other travellers who passed this way. Fittingly the churchyard has a female yew of epic proportions consisting of five 'live' stems (one cut through). The yew grows some way from the church on the eastern side and its appearance brings to mind the great yew of Llanerfyl that grows not that far away in the Banwy valley. The remains of an old stone wall surround the surviving pieces of the Llanymawddwy yew.

Near the lych gate is a mound where the stump of another big yew once stood. A further six much younger clipped yews flank the entrance path toward the church porch. As at nearby Mallwyd, the church is dedicated to the local saint Tydecho, and it is reasonable to assume that the age of this tree is similar to the largest of the Mallwyd trees.

Llangower (*Llangywer*) (SH 90423226)

Single immense yew

Due north of Llanymawddwy and north-east of Llanuwchllyn, and on either side of Llyn Tegid (Bala lake) are two sites with big old yews. On the south-western bank of the Lake by the Lake Railway and the B4403 can be found the redundant Llangower church. The double dedication of this site is to the Celtic saint Cywair from whence the place-name comes, and also to the international St George. Strikingly dominant on mounded ground on the east side of the churchyard grows a most impressive hollow female yew of great age.

In its hey-day Llangywer church was the home of an unusual bier that was transported by two horses – one at each end. It is a reminder of the days when only the horse could reach the high hill farms and cottages on roads that were unsuitable for any form of wheeled traffic. On the north side of the lake, on a narrow piece of land jutting south into the water just west of the town of Bala, is the churchyard of Llanycil. The church is dedicated to St Beuno, one of several in north Wales dedicated to this famous seventh-century saint (see Gwyddelwern, p. 70). There were eight yews recorded in the churchyard in 1833, of which five now remain. In Vaughan Cornish's 1946 publication *The Churchyard Yew and Immortality* he includes a map showing the expansion of the churchyard from its original early medieval *llan* shape. The holy well at Llanycil, *Fynnon Beuno* was referred to by the chronicler Edward Lhuyd in the eighteenth century.

Ysbyty Ifan (SH 84404890)

Three female yews growing close together

Our final visit into the Snowdonia National Park is to Ysbyty Ifan. This small village is north of both Bala and Llyn Celyn: in fact, it is on the other side of the Gylchedd Mountain (670 m), on the B4407, and has been described as 'one of the most historic places in North Wales'. The translation of the place name reads 'the pilgrim church of St John' and is the first village encountered by the infant Afon Conwy as it comes down from the mountains.

The present church stands on the site of an earlier church, very near the place where the hospice of the Knights of St John was built. It harks back to the days of medieval pilgrimage when the three holiest places in Wales were St David's (*Tyddewi*), Bardsey island (*Ynys Enlli*) and Holywell (*Treffynnon*). Ysbyty Ifan catered for the pilgrims heading to and from Bardsey. A few houses and the old stone bridge remain but even they cannot go back as far as the churchyard and its yews. Although their girths are not exceptional the trees' age is indicated by the trunks having been subject to the hollowing process. Nowadays, this village is much quieter than in former times, but these three closely growing female yews still have one another for company.

North-eastern Wales and its Borderlands

The area of the Hiraethog hills (Denbigh moors) that lie to the east of the Conwy valley has several very important yew tree sites, the most notable of which are Llangernyw and Gwytherin (see Detailed Studies).

Llangernyw (SH 87526744)
See Detailed Study, p. 39

The small village of Llangernyw is on high ground south of Abergele on the A548. The unusual dedication of the recently whitewashed church is to the fifth-century St Digain. The churchyard has pre-Christian origins, with both boulders and early inscribed stones, as well as one of Wales' greatest yew trees, a many-stemmed male tree measuring over 10 metres around the living pieces.

Gwytherin (SH 87676147)
See Detailed Study, p. 37

This remote but beautiful place on the Denbighshire moors south of Llangernyw was once an important monastic settlement. There is much recorded history from here concerning St Gwenfrewi (Winifred), her tomb and reliquary. There are also four standing stones positioned in a line on the north side of the redundant church. One has a fifth- or sixth-century Latin memorial inscription. Two of the three female churchyard yews measure over 8 metres in girth; they stand either side of the church building. Despite its isolated location Gwytherin is worth seeking out.

Pennant Melangell (SJ 02422654)
See Detailed Study, p. 43

Important site dedicated to St Melangell, with several huge yews.

Nantglyn (SJ 00416213)
Pulpit in old yew

Two further sites that are only a little less important than Llangernyw, Gwytherin and Pennant are located on the north-easterly slopes of the Clocaenog Forest. Nantglyn is positioned at the meeting of the B5435 and a minor road that makes its way over the hills from Llyn Brenig towards the town of Denbigh (*Dinbych*).

    Growing in the churchyard of St James at Nant Glyn is a 7-metre male yew with a fascinating feature. Within the hollow core of the tree, steps and a slate pulpit have been constructed. It is not known the exact point in history when the installation took place but it is known that preaching has taken place here from the Victorian period. The

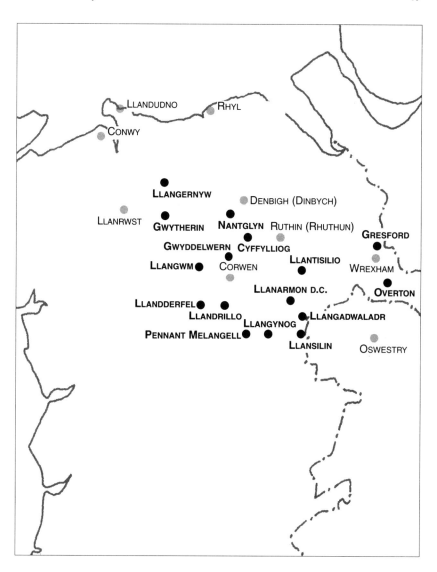

North-eastern Wales and its Borderlands

existence of the pulpit gives credence to those who believe that ancient yews were once the focal point for pagan worship and later for the proclamation of the Christian message. The yews also provided the very practical issue of shelter. This site is a 'must visit' for those who travel in this scenic area.

Cyffylliog (SJ 05905783)

Three big yews

A less well-known village lying south-east of Nant Glyn down narrow lanes with a stream close by is Cyffylliog. The redundant church of St Mary has three big yews, the largest of which is a colossal near 9-metre female tree, the only yew not growing on the churchyard's boundary. If approached from the east Cyffylliog is a short distance from Rhuthin (*Ruthun*) along narrow lanes.

Gwyddelwern (SJ 07464668)

Fragmentary remains within wall

At St Beuno's church at Gwyddelwern, north of Corwen on the A494, the damaged and heavily-pruned male yew is enclosed within a high circular wall. The tree is clearly but a fragment of a once much larger specimen. We learn from the fourteenth-century 'Life' of St Beuno that he was born of noble parents in Powys but 'operated' north of there. He established *llannau* across north Wales, his most notable site being that at the pilgrim church of Clynnog Fawr, south of Caernarfon. The place-name Gwyddelwern tells us that there was a strong Irish influence in this area for '*gwyddel*' translates as 'Irishman'. North of the village Beuno's holy well can be traced near the roadside.

Llantysilio (SJ 19404355)

Fragment of once much bigger yew

A yew of similar condition to the Gwyddelwern yew is to be seen at Llantysilio. It grows beside by the now closed church of St Tysilio on the north side of the river Dee, west of Llangollen. At first appearance the male yew looks insignificant, but on closer inspection the remains of a much larger base can be found in the ground surrounding the remaining piece. In early spring, this old churchyard is carpeted with snowdrops.

Llangwm (SH 96674460)

Two parts to solitary old yew

To the west, another sadly redundant church, although this time with a more obviously old yew, is that of St Jerome at Llangwm. It is well worth taking the trouble to visit this churchyard situated just south of the A5 to the west of Corwen. The immense female yew grows in two 'twisted' parts, with a rowan growing out of the left limb (viewed from the road). The dedication to the scholar saint, Jerome, is worth noting as Llangwm Uchaf in Monmouthshire is also dedicated to him: this church site until recently had an ancient yew.

Llandrillo (SJ 03433707)

Unmeasurable female yew

There are two sites outside the Snowdonia National Park but still in Meirionnydd. The first of these is Llandrillo, reached along the B4401 from Corwen – and what a site it is! Here behind the church of St Trillo is an unmeasurable old female yew that grows within a wide circular retaining wall. Trillo was a fifth-century saint with two dedications to his name, one on the north Wales coast and the other here in Meirionnydd. By legend St Trillo was a priest on Bardsey Island and was, like his brother Tegai, a hermit follower of the great missionary Cadfan.

The great yew at Llandrillo was depicted in a late nineteenth-century drawing by Edwin Lees. Its appearance differs little today from that 1874 drawing, other than that it now grows from two major limbs and not the three drawn by the Victorian artist. Many years ago the third limb collapsed and its remains are built into the retaining wall that surrounds the surviving parts. The tree covers a vast area and its appearance is similar in many ways to the great yew at Llanerfyl. You can say with some assurance that this yew was growing here at Llandrillo at the time the early saint was active in this part of Wales. In 1316 a bishop wrote a revealing letter concerning Llandrillo church and what was then termed 'ecclesiastical immunity'. Ecclesiastical liberty was laid out in the *Laws of Hywel Dda*, confirmed by Gerald of Wales (*Giraldus Cambrensis*) in 1188 and endorsed by the statute of Rhuddlan in 1284. The limits of sanctuary were set out by the bishops, and the boundaries were marked by fences and ditches. One Ieuan ap Madog of Edernon was charged with homicide and he sought sanctuary at Llandrillo church. Several enemies, in defiance of the immunity, led him away to Harlech Castle in the neighbouring diocese of Bangor. The bishop of St Asaph requested that Ieuan be returned. As described in the case of the maiden and the village of Miluc (see p. 25), the churchyard yew could be an integral part of the area of sanctuary.

For the lovers of all things ancient there is much to see in this fertile valley, for three prehistoric burial sites are visible from the roadsides around Llandrillo. The saint's well *Ffynnon Drillo* was noted by the eighteenth-century topographical recorder Edward Lhuyd. It was located in a field across the Afon Ceidiog from the church and was virtually dry by the turn of the twentieth century, although there is another well by the bridge in the village.

Llandderfel (SH 98163706)

Fragmentary remains of big old yew

Continuing towards Bala you reach the village of Llandderfel, and a church dedicated to the sixth-century saint Derfel. There is much history attached to both him and to the church site. According to legend, Derfel was known variously as 'Gadarn the mighty', 'Gadarn the brave', and 'the warrior saint', for he had been a soldier before taking up his missionary work, finally becoming abbot of the pilgrimage island of Bardsey (*Ynys Enlli*). Later during the middle ages a sizeable cult built up around Derfel and his holy relics, which consisted of a large wooden statue, horse and staff. It was recorded in the sixteenth century that many pilgrims visited his church, bringing livestock, clothing and money to be offered as reparation for their sins. On Easter Tuesday, and on his feast day, 5 April, up to 600 pilgrims would visit the site. Their pilgrimage would culminate in a procession following the holy relics. All this 'idolatrous' behaviour prompted the feared Thomas Cromwell to pronounce that the statue, horse and staff be taken to London for destruction, but after bribery by locals, only the statue arrived at Westminster. 'The huge and great image of Derfel' finally perished when John Forest (confessor of Catherine of Aragon), who would not renounce his faith, was ordered by Henry VIII to be burned at the gallows in Smithfield, London on 22 May 1538. Derfel's wooden statue was cut up and symbolically lit below the gallows. In *Hall's Chronicle* at the time it was written, 'now is he come with spere and shield, in harness to burne in Smithfield, for in Wales he may not dwell'. Almost 200 years later (1730) the rural dean responsible for Llanderfel ordered that the head of the surviving wooden horse be cut off and the remaining 'beast' be removed from its prominent position close to the altar. Miraculously the headless horse and staff are still 'intact' and are displayed in the church porch as a poignant reminder of a turbulent and passionate past. Also remaining on the east side of the church is the stump of one of Derfel's yews shamefully cut down within the last twenty years, although it is good to see that a young yew has been planted as a replacement. On the opposite side of the church, and surrounded by a low wall near the western boundary, the fragmentary remains of a surviving yew still grow.

Derfel's holy well, which consisted of a small bath used for curative bathing, was located over 400 metres away before its demise in the twentieth century. As if any further item of interest were needed for the village, Llandderfel was the location for a world famous UFO sighting in January 1974.

Llangynog (SJ 05302610)

Single low-branching tree

Across the Berwyn Mountains beside the B4391 in the upper Tanat valley is the Montgomeryshire village of Llangynog. The settlement is surrounded by long since abandoned quarry workings, and on higher ground, forestry plantations. The place name tells us that the church has a dedication to St Cynog, the eldest son of Brychan from Brecon (see Defynnog and Merthyr Cynog (pp. 35 and 91) for more details of his legend). The early medieval raised churchyard has a low-branching wide spreading unmeasurable yew in its south-west corner. Close inspection reveals that this yew is probably of a similar age to the yews at Pennant Melangell (see Detailed Study, p. 43) close by but further up toward the head of the Tanat valley.

Llanarmon-Dyffryn-Ceiriog (SJ 15833280)

Two big yews, one on each side of the path

There are three rewarding sites fairly close to each other on the lower slopes of the Berwyns before you reach the border town of Oswestry. The first of these is at the church of the Breton saint, Garmon, at Llanarmon-Dyffryn-Ceiriog near the head of the beautiful Ceiriog valley (B4500). In the churchyard at Llanarmon are two very big yews that grow either side of the main west path in front of the church porch and near an unexplained but distinctive 'tump', sometimes referred to as 'Garmon's Mound' on the northern side.

The small village of 'Llanarmon DC' consists of a few houses and two hostelries with good walking country all around. Cadair Berwyn (823 m) and Cadair Bronwen rise up on the west; down the Ceiriog at Pontfadog one of Britain's mightiest oaks grows on the valley side.

Llangadwaladr (SJ 18163036)

Line of yews on an old boundary

To the south-east in remote hill country is the big rural parish of Llangadwaladr. Between a brook and a narrow lane is the isolated single-chambered church dedicated to St Cadwaladr, an early saint with a well-known church site on Anglesey (*Ynys Môn*). Here in border country a line of old yews grows on a low ridge, probably the original enclosure bank of the churchyard. The largest yew of the line is a female tree measuring over 7 metres.

Llansilin (SJ 20962819)

Six yews, all big

Few churchyards can boast so many big yews as Llansilin. No fewer than six old trees grow around St Silin's church, which is at the heart of this attractive village due west of Oswestry on the B4580. Two of the male yews are over 8 metres, the larger of them to the south-east of the church building. The yews certainly impressed the travel writer George Borrow, who visited the churchyard in 1854 and wrote of the 'several enormous yew trees' in his chronicle *Wild Wales*.

Gresford (*Gresffordd*) (SJ 34645497)

Many yews, but only one ancient specimen

The two remaining churchyards chosen for inclusion from this region are both close to the English border and both have well documented histories. The very large churchyard at Gresford (B5445), positioned on low-lying land north of Wrexham in an area once famed for its coal mining, boasts one of Wales' finest churches. Not unsurprisingly, with its proximity to the border it is very English in style, with its wealth derived from pilgrims visiting the once well-known shrine to St Mary. As a result of this the church was able to gain considerable wealthy patronage, evident aurally in the famous 'peal of bells'. Surrounding the church are many yews planted in the early eighteenth century. One further yew to the south-east of the church building can, however, claim to be truly ancient. Its existence gives us an indication of the origins of the site, from the time when an early saints' cell probably existed in pre-conquest days long before the fine church was built. A substantial Victorian iron railing surrounds this huge 9-metre male. Further evidence of the antiquity of the site was unearthed in Victorian times during work on the boiler house, when a remarkable Romano-British inscribed stone was found. It is displayed on the floor in the south aisle and commemorates 'Marta – shears which cut the thread of life'. It is believed offerings to her were placed in the hollow on the stone's top.

A more recent and tragic commemoration is the memorial to the 266 miners of Gresford colliery who perished in the mining disaster of September 1934.

Overton (SJ 37354181)

Yews amongst the 'Seven Wonders of Wales'

On the southern side of Wrexham and on a piece of Wales that 'juts out' towards the north Shropshire plain is the attractive village of Overton (*Owrtyn*). The place-name in old English reads 'river bank settlement', and indeed the river Dee flows nearby to the west. Overton is home to one of the 'Seven Wonders of Wales', namely the churchyard yews. As at Gresford, of the many yews on site only one can be considered of great age; this male tree is a mere 'shell'. It, too, has a railing, but this time it is a modern installation funded by a grant aid scheme. The 'modern' work also involved the addition of tree props and the diversion of a footpath from around the base of the yew (near the north-west lych gate).

The forester R. T. Wheeler surveyed the Overton yews in 1984 and recorded twenty-two trees: sixteen female, five male and a young yew of undetermined sex. Since then a 'millennium' yew has been added. Wheeler also assessed the possible age of the old male tree using annual ring counts from bits of decaying heartwood. He came up with a figure of between 750 and 1000 years of age. In 1993 a piece of heartwood from the same tree was radio-carbon dated by Oxford University Archaeology Unit. The results proved both disappointing and inconclusive and came up with a possible age range for the tree of 'at least four hundred, and possibly over six hundred and fifty years'. The difficulty of using carbon dating methods on ancient yews is covered in the chapter on 'Measuring and Ageing Yews'. Regardless of these 'ageing' attempts Overton has much to offer the curious passer-by.

Central Wales – north

This region covers the Vale of the Severn that heads in a north-easterly direction from Llanidloes towards the English border near Shrewsbury. Some sites on or near the river Banwy also feature, as well as a cluster around Machynlleth outside the Snowdonia National Park.

Buttington (SJ 2980884)

Largest yew is 1200 years old (by tradition)

To the east of Welshpool runs the river Severn, and just above the flood plain and beside the A458 Shrewsbury road lies Buttington. The small community has a pretty whitewashed church (All Saints) and in the south-west corner of the churchyard an 8-metre-girthed male yew grows. The tree's bole looks solid but a narrow crack reveals it is almost completely hollow. The yew must have borne witness to the building of the schoolhouse in the corner of the churchyard in 1838. When excavation for this building took place many skulls were unearthed, causing speculation that this was the site of the legendary Battle of Buttington. More recent research largely discounts this theory, suggesting that the skulls may be from the time of the great plague.

Guilsfield (*Cegidfa*) (SJ 21921165)

Twenty-two yews, one with planting date

Across the valley on the B4392 at Guilsfield (Cegidfa) is a churchyard with no fewer than twenty-two yews, none of them ancient. Most of them were planted in the late seventeenth or early eighteenth centuries. Of interest here is the female yew located to the left of the entrance path close to the gate, which was planted by a Richard Jones in the company of his father when Richard was but a boy. In 1707, aged ninety, he was buried below the yew, and his tombstone is marked with a skull and cross-bones. An approximate planting date of 1625 indicates that even a yew of this size, which looks small in comparison to many others, is around 400 years old (see p. 118). The first church at Guilsfield was built towards the end of the sixth century, a long time before the present church, which displays many interesting features including a hearse house built in 1739, and some excellent woodcraft. The church is dedicated to St Aelhaiarn, one of three brothers, all Christian missionaries, and Aelhaiarn's holy well is at a nearby roadside.

Manafon (SJ 11300247)

Two yews

Manafon churchyard is beside the small river Rhiw and the B4390 south-west of Welshpool. It has two big yews that have been heavily pruned back in the past. The largest is the female tree growing from two distinct stems close to the lych gate. It was recorded as being a large tree in 1849. The great twentieth-century poet R S Thomas was once rector at Manafon.

Travelling across central Wales in a westerly direction from Welshpool to Mallwyd there are several good yew tree sites. After leaving Welshpool and the Severn valley on the age-old route that cuts across towards southern Merionydd you pass the north side of the great Powis estate as you gradually rise into the heart of central Wales.

Llangynyw (SJ 12710909)

Four old yews

The first selected yew site to be encountered is at the church of St Cynyw at Llangynyw. This large rural parish of few dwellings sits amidst rolling farmland north-east of Llanfair Caereinion. The lovely church sits alone on high ground, just north of the A458. Its dominant oak porch contrasts starkly with the whitewashed walls of the church and the dark green, almost black, old yews that surround it. Of these fine trees, four appear older than the others. Most of the yews are female but the largest is a male growing on sloping ground on the opposite side of the church from the main gate. Behind the church the enclosure has been extended to accommodate new burials, but the old yews show us the original boundary of the *llan*.

Back on the A458 heading west look out for a surviving big old wych-elm growing beside the north side of the road just before reaching Llanfair Caereinion. It is at Llanfair that the light railway that heads up the valley from Welshpool finishes its journey. This popular attraction affords the passengers lovely views over the gradually ascending landscape of Montgomeryshire.

Llanerfyl (SJ 03400977)

See Detailed Study p. 41

No yew in this region or in fact in the whole of Wales can compare with the churchyard yew at Llanerfyl. The way the broken and twisted tree has spread itself out over the churchyard in front of the porch is extraordinary. The village of Llanerfyl is west of Llangynyw, just before the A458 crosses the Afon Banwy via a narrow old bridge, before reaching Llangadfan and the Cann Office Hotel.

Beyond Foel and visible high above the main road on the northern side is the church of St Tydecho at Garthbeibio. This Celtic saint established his small cult in this area in the sixth century, with Mallwyd and Llanymawddwy, close by in Merionnydd. The two sites have significant yews and the old split female yew at Garthbeibio is probably far older than its 7-metre girth suggests. This yew was listed in 1946 as one of significance and it grows north-east of the church. The partial remains of a further old yew are by the porch and path on the south side. The holy well of Tydecho, recorded in 1796, was near the church and contained a stone image of the saint's head. Unfortunately the well was filled in sometime in the twentieth century.

Carno (SN 96329648)

Impressive yew

Another of the main routes linking England to west Wales travels along the valley now carrying the A470. Midway along this road between Newtown and Machynlleth you

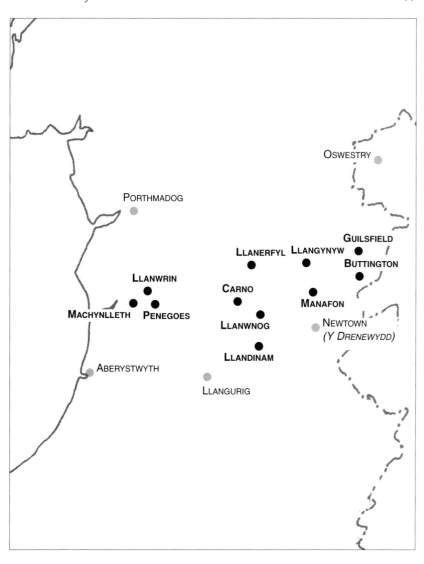

Central Wales – north

reach Carno. The church of St John the Baptist at Carno contains an early medieval cross slab moved from a nearby farm where it was being used as a gatepost until 1960. It is an indication of the early Christian presence hereabouts. The church has associations with the Knights Hospitallers, who according to the chronicler Pennant, owned the church in the thirteenth century. A more modern association is with the designer and entrepreneur Laura Ashley, who set up her first studio at Carno. She was a benefactor of the church and is buried in the churchyard.

West of the church near the entrance gate a beautifully fluted but hollow female yew grows to over 7 metres. This elegant low-crowned tree has the support of a metal bar as part of remedial tree surgery operations. An internal stem grows ever stouter within the yew's hollow core.

Llanwrin (SH 78660353)

Regrowth from cuts

Continuing westwards and after meeting the A489 at Cemmaes Road (*Glantwymyn*) a minor road crosses the Afon Dyfi and travels along its western banks (B4404). The only settlement of any size along this scenic road is Llanwrin, and here to the north is the church of St Gwrin. Historically the church is believed to be a re-dedication from the dual saints Ust and Dyfrig. Credence to this is given by the old field name nearby, which translates as 'the field of the three saints'. The churchyard is of much antiquity, highlighted by the extraordinary male yew growing to the west of the present church. At first appearance, the yew looks modest with a small compact crown, but when inspected at close quarters the enormity and age of the old base become apparent. Severe pruning almost destroyed the tree in the 1980s, and in fact the yew was described as being 'dead' in 1984. The great powers of re-growth of the yew species are amply demonstrated by the Llanwrin tree, but the close proximity of a line of dwellings may be the reason for continued pruning works.

Llanwrin features in one of the Welsh folk tales collected by William Wirt Sykes, the American novelist and journalist. A story in his book *British Goblins: Welsh folklore, fairy mythology, legends and traditions*, published in 1880, tells of fairy activity in Ffridd yr Ywen, a wood in the Parish of Llanwrin, in the centre of which grew a magical yew tree.

Machynlleth (SH 74530095)

Yew with three main stems

At Machynlleth, where in 1404 Owain Glyndŵr convened the last independent Welsh parliament, the parish church of St Peter takes up a dominant position in this historic town. The original dedication of the church was probably to St Cybi. In the large churchyard there is an ancient male yew that grows to the east of the slate grey church. This unmeasurable old tree is often disregarded, as all that is visible above ground are three relatively young stems growing out of the original root system.

Penegoes (SH 76840093)

Giant male yew

A few miles east of Machynlleth on the ancient route over the Felin Gerrig bridge, the busy A48 reaches Penegoes. The church is dedicated to St Cadfarch (and in fact the old name for the village is Llangadfarch). Here at the east end of the churchyard is a giant male yew measuring over 9 metres around its surviving portions. The antiquity of the area is demonstrated by the recording of two holy wells in the parish. One of the wells had the name *Ffynnon Gadfarch* and was located opposite the old schoolhouse. Until 1904 it was maintained by the rector as part of his duties. The holy well has been restored several times in recent decades, but rural wells need regular maintenance or they soon fall into disrepair. The place name Penegoes is believed to mean 'head of Egoes' who was either a mythical chieftain or an early saint. Whichever he was, his head is said to be buried beneath some nearby oaks.

Penegoes sits at the head of no fewer than five valleys and must have been a place of great strategic importance in bygone days. The village's most famous son was the landscape artist Richard Wilson (1713-82), who was educated by his parents at the rectory. He went on to study in Italy and became noted for depicting many familiar British landscapes. He was also a founder of the Royal Academy, and a memorial to him is sited in Penegoes church.

Llandinam (SO 02648860)

Yew 800 years old, by tradition

It is easy to miss the church and churchyard of St Llonio at Llandinam: they sit on high ground above the road and river Severn (*Afon Hafren*) south-west of Newtown on the A470. It would be a pity to miss them, as the 'church on the fort' is a special place. It was once a *clas* site or 'mother church' to several others, including that in the now much larger town of Llanidloes. St Llonio was a monk at Bangor before starting his missionary work in this part of Wales. The long wedge-shaped churchyard is widest at the top by the church and narrows as it dips towards the river. An old, good-looking three-stemmed female yew grows midway down the slope, and consists of younger growth from the original piece. It is surrounded by a wall, and by local tradition is 800 years old. By all appearances this is a modest assessment.

Llanwnog (SO 02239382)

Nine yews

North of Llandinam and between Newtown and Carno there is a minor road on the north side of the valley (B4568) that goes through the village of Llanwnog. Here the seldom-visited churchyard is adorned with no fewer than nine yews, several of which are of some considerable age. Of particular note are the two trees growing either side of the path near the east gate. The female yew to the north is narrowly the larger. The church is dedicated to St Gwynnog (reputedly the son of Gildas), who emigrated to Brittany after finishing his missionary work in Wales.

Central Wales – south

This region is largely made up of what was once the old administrative county of Radnorshire, a county characterised by its pleasant rolling hills that rise and dip on the western side of King Offa's famous dyke.

Disgoed (SO 27666474)

Two large yews

Near the small border town of Presteigne (*Llanandras*), there are a number of good yew sites, with Disgoed to the west being one of the best. The settlement is between the B4356 and the B4357, on a minor road. At Disgoed's St Michael's churchyard are two substantial yews, one on the south-western boundary; the other, a male tree, to the north. This specimen has received much attention lately, with claims of an age exceeding 4,000 years being made. Although very large, the tree is mainly made up of many stems growing out of a split base. This has the effect of exaggerating the girth measurement and gives rise to the inflated age estimation. At its narrowest it can be measured between 8 and 9 metres, measured only slightly higher from the ground at over 11 metres. Arriving at an age estimation from girth on this yew is nigh on impossible (see p. 18). Unusually this tree has a very narrow crown when viewed from one direction and very wide from another. Whichever way it is viewed it is a very impressive tree.

Just outside the entrance gate is an old well, and the whole feeling of the location is one of antiquity.

Further down the lane towards the B4357 and next to Offa's Dyke is another very large old yew by the appropriately named Yew Tree Farm.

Casgob (SO 23906639)

One huge yew

Continuing west after crossing the B4357 and onto an even more minor road that – though difficult to believe – was once a highway toward London, you reach the settlement that sits below the upland area of Radnor Forest. As with Disgoed, the church at Casgob is dedicated St Michael, one of several in this area, only this time 'All Saints' has been added. Casgob's place-name is early Saxon and the settlement was probably a Saxon enclave before the building of Offa's dyke (see chapter on 'The History of the Early Church in Wales'). At one time this large churchyard was thought to have been built on top of a pre-Christian burial mound but recent excavations have largely discounted this theory. The pronounced 'tump' near the church tower is nothing more than grassed-over rubble from church restoration work, and not Bronze Age workings as was originally thought. The churchyard is home to a good-looking clean-boled female yew, which really is a gem. It grows with a large even-spreading crown to the south-west of the church and is 7 metres round.

Inside the church on the north wall of the nave hangs a framed parchment dug up long ago outside the church building. It is a written 'abracadabra' charm dated to 1700,

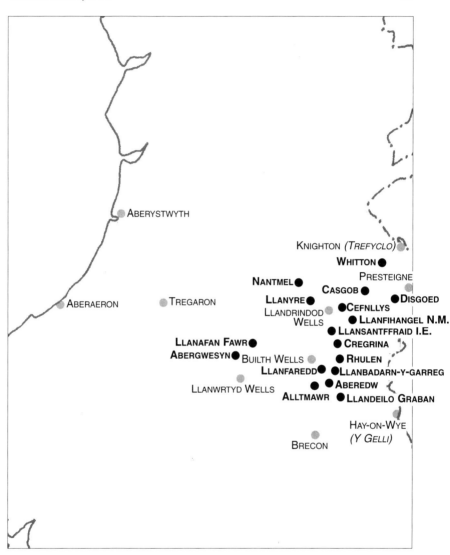

ABERYSTWYTH

KNIGHTON *(TREFYCLO)*

WHITTON ●

PRESTEIGNE

NANTMEL ●

CASGOB ●

●DISGOED

LLANYRE ●

●CEFNLLYS

LLANDRINDOD
WELLS

● LLANFIHANGEL N.M.

● LLANSANTFFRAID I.E.

LLANAFAN FAWR ●

● CREGRINA

ABERGWESYN ●

BUILTH WELLS

● RHULEN

LLANFAREDD ●

●LLANBADARN-Y-GARREG

LLANWRTYD WELLS

● ABEREDW

ALLTMAWR ●

● LLANDEILO GRABAN

HAY-ON-WYE
(Y GELLI)

BRECON

ABERAERON

TREGARON

Central Wales – south

and designed to drive out evil spirits thought to have beset Elizabeth Lloyd, a female parishioner. This is an example of earlier beliefs mixing with the Christian, not an unusual occurrence in eighteenth-century rural areas. Unusually for a churchyard, an old apple tree grows on the 'tump' near the tower and several big old conifers adorn the surroundings.

Whitton (SO 27056733)

Several big yews

Closer to Presteigne by the river Lugg and the junction of the B4356 and B4357 is Whitton churchyard, where several big yews grow by St David's church. They are difficult to get close to in the summer months due to the growth of high vegetation. The biggest yew is a male measuring over 7 metres. A huge redwood tree used to grow by the entrance gate. It has recently been felled but the impressive stump remains (2007).

There is a band of folk who visit all the Radnorshire churches with a St Michael dedication. These modern 'pilgrims' are drawn to these sites for, according to legend, it was St Michael who 'kept the churches safe' from the fearsome dragon who roamed and terrorised the Radnor Forest in the Middle Ages.

Llanfihangel Nant Melan (SO 18015818)

Five yews on old bank

On the visit list is the church and churchyard at Llanfihangel Nant Melan. This village is beside the Summergill Brook in wild mountain country between Presteigne and Builth Wells on the A44 mid-Wales route. In the twelfth century the church was given to the Knights Hospitallers; tradition relates that it is set within the ring of a now-disappeared stone circle. This image is reinforced by the yews that grow on the old boundary, one of which has within its base a boulder now partly grown over by the tree's roots. Only archaeological work, which is unlikely to take place, can possibly confirm early history, so we are left to muse on legends, traditions and conjecture. Many yews were once recorded, but now only five remain: the biggest, a split tree, is south-west of the church and measures over 8 metres.

Cefnllys (SO 08476150)

Several old yews at remote site

There are three sites within striking distance of Llandrindod Wells, the first on the east of the town. A lane takes you out of the suburbs and into the countryside and down to the 'Shaky Bridge' that spans the Afon Ithon. The bridge retains its name from the time when it was a rickety old wooden structure. It is now much sturdier and more substantial, with a car parking spot close by the riverbank and adjacent woodland.

Cefnllys is another of the St Michael churches, and is reached after crossing the Shaky Bridge and following the path to the left skirting Cefnllys Hill then reaching the circular churchyard. In the Middle Ages the large hill had a castle on top and a village stood on the meadows below the church. Now the church sits alone protected by its dark yew trees, of which the male tree to the south-east has a 6-metre girth. On the

Castle Hill's steep side grows a wild yew by a rocky outcrop – probably a seedling from the older churchyard trees.

Cefnllys is a beautiful spot and walks can be enjoyed all around and along the quiet Ithon.

Llanyre (SO 04456231)

Four old yews

Two miles north-west of Llandrindod Wells on a minor road between the A4081 and A44 is the village of Llanyre, its name derived from the obscure fifth-century saint Llyr. It is not known for certain whether this Llyr was male, or the female virgin saint associated with Llanllŷr, a former nunnery in Cardigan.

Of the four big yews in the small churchyard the largest is a male tree on the north side of the church and measuring over 7 metres. Llanyre churchyard is supposedly built on top of a Bronze Age barrow: this has not as yet been confirmed by archaeological research.

Nantmel (SO 03436637)

Ring of old yews

The last of the yew tree sites recommended in these parts is the 'mother church' to Llanyre at Nantmel. Situated just above the A44 between Cross Gates and Rhaeadr, the curved and embanked churchyard, first consecrated in the sixth century by St Cynllo (as with Llanbister) is a gem. Steep stone steps lead up to the church and well-tended burial ground that faces southwards towards the River Dulas. The churchyard has a semi-circle of yews on the south and south-eastern sides, with historical reference to the trees from 1818. Of the big yews on the southern boundary a female tree measures in excess of 8 metres, giving authenticity to the claims of a pre-conquest establishment at Nantmel.

Llanafan Fawr (SN 96915578)

Many-stemmed huge yew

One of the most impressive yews in Wales can be found further south-west of Llandrindod Wells and Newbridge-on-Wye at Llanafan Fawr. The roller-coaster ride that is the B4358 runs along the old Roman route between Newbridge and Beulah on the lower slopes of the great Cambrian uplands, with the Chwefri river below. Eventually the Chwefri runs into the Irfon before reaching the river Wye (*Afon Gwy*) at Builth Wells. Opposite the well known historic cruck-framed hostelry, The Red Lion, is the equally historic but far older churchyard that surrounds St Afan's church. There is much here to satisfy the historian.

Afan was supposedly a cousin of St David, and the stone named St Afan's 'tomb' that carries a thirteenth- or fourteenth-century inscription is situated on the site. Legends dictate that the stone marks the spot where St Afan was slain by either Irish or Danish invaders. Set in the east wall of the porch are fragments of ninth-century patterned stonework, probably by Irish or Irish-inspired craftsmen. The Irish may well have had an early monastic centre at Llanafan Fawr. The early medieval theme is continued in the church, where near the altar is an inscribed stone, which has been dated at between the seventh and ninth centuries. The whole feeling of the churchyard is one of antiquity, endorsed by local place-names such as 'The Saint's Bush' (*Perth y Sant*), 'Afan's Oak' (*Derwen Afan*), 'Bishop's Valley' (*Cwm Esgob*) and 'Bishop's Stream' (*Nant yr Sgob*). Two holy wells, *Ffynnon Afan* and *Ffynnon Dduw*, have also been recorded.

Of great interest to the yew tree enthusiast is the huge bulk of the giant female yew that grows on the eastern side of the narrow church, just below a flat platform of land that looks to have once borne an ecclesiastical building. The base of the yew is a tangle of thick stems that have re-grown over many centuries, somewhat reminiscent of the famous Ashbrittle Yew in Devon. The measurement around all living and dead parts exceeds 10 metres. Outside of this ring of stems are younger yews of varying size, age and sex: these will be seedlings from the mother tree. This yew surely goes back to the very origins of the Christian site at Llanafan, and will have witnessed all the passions and tribulations of the many people and their activities. The scene today is one of solitude and tranquillity.

Abergwesyn (SN 85405268)

Approached from either Beulah or Llantwrtyd Wells, and set amid the forest plantations and recreational areas of the Tywi Forest, is the locality of Abergwesyn. On either side of the Irfon bridge, just before the Afon Gwesyn joins the bigger river, are two deserted church sites, Llanddewi Abergwesyn (St David) near the west bank of the river and Llanfihangel Abergwesyn (St Michael) to the east.

One yew at deserted site

St David's church, standing as recently as 1969, contained an early inscribed stone, and part of a Roman altar built into the frame of the church. All that is now left as a poignant reminder of the ecclesiastical past is the lonely 6-metre female yew, with a rather misshapen male offspring of the big old tree cowering a few feet away below its crown.

Seven yews clustered around site of old church

Across the bridge and close to the road is the spot where St Michael's church once stood; the churchyard is still used for the occasional burial. A large fairly modern Celtic cross stands between five male yews. On a steep bank beside the road is a striking example of the phenomenon of a yew developing into a dual-sex tree, with the female portion growing closest to the road. In all there are six old yews at St Michael's.

The whole area around Abergwesyn is a delight well worth taking the diversion away from the main A483 route to explore. For those with a high sense of adventure and visiting in the summer, there is a spectacular mountain road over the wild uplands to the west, eventually reaching Tregaron in Ceredigion.

Llansantffraed in Elvel (*Llansanffraed-yn-Elfael*) (SO 9965486)

Many old yews

The hills of Radnorshire to the south and east of Builth Wells (*Llanfair-ym-muallt*) are rich indeed in ancient churchyard yews. Four miles down the A481 and on the north side of the road lies Llansantffraed in Elvel. As the name implies it has a church dedicated to St Brigid, usually the sign of early Irish influence in the area. Brigid of Kildare, as far as we are aware, never visited nor founded any churches herself in Wales – they were set up by followers of her cult, which dates in Wales from the fifth and sixth centuries. Foundations are normally found in rich fertile valleys good for the growing of crops. In the twelfth century Llansanffraed was the site of a Cistercian nunnery. The churchyard has been considerably enlarged over time from its original small circular form, and contains many yews of different ages and shapes. A 7-metre male tree with a pronounced mound around its base grows to the south-west. Behind the church a group of yews appear to grow from one huge old base, but on closer inspection they can be seen to be both male and female and so are probably seedlings. However, it is always worth checking these 'younger' trees as they may be re-growths from an old forgotten 'ancient'.

Llanfaredd (SO 06955075)

Huge female yew

A group of no fewer than six churchyards with ancient yews are east of the Wye and Builth Wells between the A481 and the B4594. The first to be encountered, travelling down the east side of the River Wye, is Llanfaredd, with a church dedication to St Mary. On the western boundary of the small churchyard is a huge female yew of over 9 metres, reputed by some to be 3,000 years old. The forgotten holy well associated with the church site lay further up the slopes of Aberedw Hill.

Aberedw (SO 08024731)

Several yews

The village of Aberedw is further down the Wye just before the Afon Edw joins the main river under the B4567. In the churchyard either side of the path grow a male and a female yew, and in days gone by dancing took place between these trees. A feature of the fourteenth- or fifteenth-century church is the unusually dominant porch where, in the not too distant past, musicians perched on the double tiers of stone benches and played for the dancers. The porch was also used on feast and festival days by itinerant merchants selling their wares. The church is dedicated to the sixth-century St Cewydd – 'old Cewydd of the rain'– the Celtic equivalent of the Saxon St Swithun, and it is located high above the fast flowing Edw. A short distance away a footpath leads to the cave of Llywelyn ap Gruffudd, a famous Welsh hero. Tradition tells of his murder after attending Mass at Aberedw. This whole area is criss-crossed by footpaths with panoramic views.

Llanbadarn-y-garreg (SO 11254877)

Two yews

Moving east along the Edw you soon come across, on your left, the whitewashed and primitive thirteenth-century church of St Padarn at Llanbadarn-y-garreg. Padarn was a fifth- or sixth-century saint who came out of the Llancarfan 'school' in south-east Wales; he founded the abbey at Llanbadarn Fawr near Aberystwyth. Most of the churches dedicated to him are beside Roman routes. This church at a peaceful spot by the Edw contains two yews, with the leaning male tree in the west corner probably the older. Within this tree's hollow core a 'classic' internal stem grows.

Rhulen (*Rhiwlen*) (SO 13774984)

Yews on east and south boundaries

The landscape now becomes wilder and less accessible, and after some twists and turns you reach the settlement of Rhulen, an atmospheric place on one of the old drovers' routes to Paincastle. All around, the curved hills look down to this special spot.

The mounded circular churchyard has all the appearance of an early burial site, reinforced by the line of six boundary yews growing above a stream to the south and east. The simple, unmodernised whitewashed church of St David is late Norman. The church history informs us that at some time in the fourteenth century an extension to the chancel was curtailed 'because of a yew tree growing'. This tree was felled only in recent times (the stump still remains). The original dedication at Rhulen was probably to St Tillo as there is a *Cwm Tillo* close by.

Cregrina (SO 12365210)

Two old yews

A mile and a half north-west of Rhulen brings us to Cregrina, and to another church that was on a main drovers' route. This is another whitewashed church dedicated to St David (although unlike Rhulen it has been updated at different periods of its history). The church was first mentioned in 1291, but now only the nave and font show their original Norman form. At this secluded site above the Edw the two big male churchyard yews stand opposite the west wall, the one nearer the church having a noticeably hollow trunk.

Llandeilo Graban (SO 09374468)

Three old yews

Retracing your way back down the Afon Edw and out to the east bank of the Wye heading south down the B4567, you have above you the dramatic ridges of Aberedw Rocks. Eventually, rather than cross the Wye at Erwood Bridge, you climb up the hill by a series of sharp, steep bends until you see a turn to the west and Llandeilo Graban is reached, from where on a clear day glorious views over towards the Brecon Beacons are revealed. In the churchyard are three impressive old yews, the biggest, growing south-west of the church is a male tree measuring just below 8 metres. The church dedication is to Teilo of Llandeilo Fawr, one of Wales' most celebrated early saints. This is the only Teilo dedication in Radnorshire. Several local features have 'Teilo-attached' names, including St Teilo's Barn and St Teilo's Pool, both to the north towards Llandeilo Hill.

Alltmawr (SO 07344687)

Very big yew in small churchyard

The final churchyard chosen from the many good sites in this region is probably the most difficult to find. Although it is but a stone's throw from Aberedw, the river Wye separates them and the nearest bridges are either south at Erwood or north at Builth Wells.

Alltmawr is a tiny settlement with an equally tiny church and churchyard – in fact the latter is reputedly the smallest in Wales. Not sign-posted from the main A470 trunk road, it lies somewhat significantly directly across the Wye from Aberedw, and is approached from a rising track on the west side after passing Abernant (coming from the south). This unique site includes the unusual dedication to the international saint, Mauritius. The huge solitary male yew grows on a bank just below the track and entrance gate, and measures almost 9 metres. Although awkward to find, the visit to this site is worth the effort.

To leave Alltmawr, it is necessary to negotiate the farmyard and its gates then back down to the main road (recommended), or you could retrace the track back south: this manoeuvre is not easy because of getting out on to the main road! Above the church and to the west is hill country, and beyond Alltmawr Uchaf is the line of the long distance path, the Wye Valley Walk.

The Brecon Region

A wealth of good yew sites occur within and around the Brecon Beacons National Park (*Parc Genedlaethol Brycheiniog*), an area that covers not only the Beacons themselves but the upper Usk (*Wysg*) valley and the Black Mountains.

Aberllynfi (SO 17303081)

Hollow yew

Entering Wales from the border town of Hay-on-Wye (*Y Gelli Gandryll*) you follow the river to its crossing at Glasbury (*Clas-ar-Wy*), and soon afterwards Aberllynfi is reached. The famous old inn, the Three Cocks, which gives the locality its English name, is now the haunt of the angler and tourist, but was once an important staging post. The name derives not from a fowl but from the 'cock horse' – the additional horse added to lead the team in their ascent up the steep hills towards Brecon.

Close to the inn, the deserted church site of Aberllynfi can be approached by footpath from either Glasbury or from behind some holiday cottages located off the A4079. The medieval church was abandoned in the late eighteenth century, and an old male yew measuring just below 6 metres is the only remaining feature of this once thriving ecclesiastical centre. There is now no sign of the church building and the yew must be viewed from a public path as it now grows on private land.

Bronllys, a little further along the A438 has a church with a detached tower – a rarity in Wales. In past times the tower was used as a potential refuge in times of siege. Livestock would be kept at ground floor level and the most vulnerable of the village inhabitants would hide on the first floor. The main yew interest at Bronllys is a tree that displays a similar weeping wound to the 'bleeding yew' of Nevern (*Nyfer*) (see p. 110). This tree grows on the right-hand side leading from the lych gate, with the 'issuing' branch overhanging the path.

Talgarth (SO 15733382)

Spreading yew and others

South of Bronllys, at Talgarth, the big churchyard is located up a hill in the old heart of the small town. The largest yew, close to the boundary wall, divides low down and forms a wide-spreading crown. It is a female tree measuring over 7 metres below the division. Talgarth church is dedicated to St Gwendoline, who was believed to be one of the many daughters of Brychan (the first king of Brecon after the departure of the Romans, and the founder of a long line of saints); tradition says she is buried in the churchyard.

There is also a memorial here to Howell Harris (1714-73), one of the founders of Welsh Calvinistic Methodism.

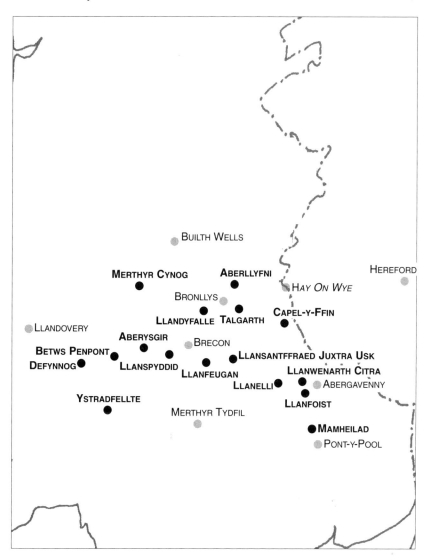

The Brecon Region

Llandyfalle (SO 10733549)

Several yews

North of Talgarth and west of Bronllys and reached by a narrow byway off the A470 is the community of Llandyfalle. Here the large, recently whitewashed (2008) church of St Matthew stands on sloping ground at the top of a steep lane. The original dedication was to the Celtic saint Maelog, so an early medieval foundation is probable for this hidden site that looks out towards the Black Mountains to the south. Just visible on the church's north wall are the remains of the old iron hinges and stays, a reminder of days gone by when shutters were used to protect the windows from ball players who used this part of the churchyard as a playground.

Of the several big old yews around the churchyard at Llandyfalle a hollow female tree is the largest. By the path on the south side of the church a male yew grows to almost the same size. The largest yew was probably the one whose stump remains amidst the gravestones east of the church building. There are other younger yews adorning the churchyard landcape.

Llanspyddid (*Llansbyddyd*) (SO 01192818)

Eight old yews

West of Brecon itself and following the A40 along the higher reaches of the Usk you come across several more yew sites. The first of these is on the south side of the main road but still close to Brecon and is the most important early medieval churchyard at Llanspyddid. This is reputedly the burial place of Brychan's father Anlach, an Irish prince. A late seventh- or early eighth-century inscribed stone known as 'The Cross of Brychan Brycheiniog' is associated with Anlach, and this early gravestone is now positioned rather incongruously amongst modern headstones behind the church. The church dedication is to St Cattwg (Cadog), Anlach's grandson.

Of the eight yews here, several are very old, bordering on ancient, with the oldest – possibly the original 'saint's tree' – a huge hulk in the north-west corner to the right of the entrance gate on the present boundary. This female tree measures in excess of 8 metres. Despite its closeness to the busy trunk road, a convenient pull-in allows easy access to this sacred spot that still retains a special atmosphere.

Aberysgir (SO 00042966)

Two old yews

Off a quiet farm lane north of Llanspyddid and the river Usk and next to the Roman remains at Y Gaer is the church at Aberysgir. There is a double dedication (SS Cynidr and Mary) and an ancient yew for each saint: for growing either side of the path on the north side of the church are two big female yews. One has a distinctive internal stem, the other is very hollow, but they are of a similar age and measure over 6 metres.

Betws Penpont (SN 97252928)

Over thirty yews

Abutting the north side of the A40, between the road and the Usk, is the unusual site of Betws Penpont: not only is the church undedicated but it has an unusual round tower. There are also no fewer than thirty yews growing in the ill-defined churchyard north of the church. The antiquity of the site is given away by the large handsome 8-metre male yew growing close to the north-eastern corner of the building. The younger yews, it is reported, replaced an older circle of trees, and according to records a second ancient yew was felled in the 1970s.

Defynnog (SN 92542793)

See Detailed Study

Whilst encouraging the yew enthusiast to visit as many of these sites as possible, there is in this area one unmissable churchyard, that at Defynnog. Defynnog has it all – ancient yews, a clas site, an inscribed stone with pre- and early Christian markings, and a saint's legend (St Cynog). The village is strategically placed at the junction of three routes: two lead through the Brecon Beacons (one to Ystradgynlais (A4067), the other to link with the A470 Merthyr Tydfil road), and the third lies just to the north (A40) following the upper Usk on the old route to west Wales.

Merthyr Cynog (SN 98483745)

Mature yews and younger growth

Cynog was the illegitimate son of Brychan, and as well as at Defynnog another very old dedication to him is located up the Afon Ysgir valley north-west of Brecon at Merthyr Cynog. The prefix Merthyr tells us that this is the reputed resting place of the saint (martyr). Giraldus Cambrensis wrote in the twelfth century that Cynog's famous torque, revered as an amulet (protector) by the local population, was shown to him when he visited the village in the twelfth century. The curvilinear churchyard is on high ground, and as with Defynnog was originally a *clas* site. There is a record from 1702 of two churches in the parish, both with dedications to Cynog, one of them a ruin with 'yew trees about'. There are several yews growing today in the present churchyard. The biggest, a male tree by the southern entrance, now has a piece split from its main trunk. To the north-east and growing to the right of the path going away from the church is a collection of yews all of the male sex. (There is also a yew stump with them.) One speculates whether they all grow from the same root system. If this were so they would measure almost 14 metres! It is an intriguing thought, but as with Defynnog, only more detailed work can confirm whether this is the case or not.

Llanfeugan (SO 08672453)

Twelve big yews

Travelling down the western side of the river Usk from Brecon (B4558) you soon come to Pencelli where a castle used to protect the river crossing. To the west of the village in the eastern foothills of the Brecon Beacons is a remote church site that stands alone with no community around it. This is Llanfeugan (also spelt Llanfigan, Llanveugan and several other versions), and the church is dedicated to the local saint Meugan, whose poetry is included in the mid thirteenth-century *Black Book of Carmarthen*, the earliest surviving document written in Welsh. Saints' legends inform us that Meugan predated St David, and that along with many other Welsh saints Meugan's final resting place was at Bardsey (*Ynys Enlli*), an island off the Llŷn Peninsula in north-west Wales. The long raised churchyard at Llanfeugan is a 'squeezed' circular shape and is dominated by no fewer than twelve big yews. The two largest and oldest grow above steep ground on the north-east side, and one of these is a female of over 9 metres.

Llansantffraed-juxta-Usk (SO 12242349)

One old yew

Further south at Talybont a road bridge crosses the Usk to join the old Roman route that now carries the A40. Here right by the banks of the river is Llansantffraed-juxta-Usk. As the name implies the settlement and early medieval church site are connected with St Brigid (Brigid) and like Llansanffraed-yn-Elfael there is an impressive ancient yew. Brigid was rather romantically known in these parts as 'the Celtic spirit of the hills'. The churchyard yew is a male tree measuring over 7 metres and growing to the south-east of the church.

The village, previously known as 'anglicised' Newton (still named on some maps), was the early home of the renowned seventeenth-century Vaughan twins. Thomas was a mystic and alchemist and for a long time rector at Llansanffraed before being banished by the puritans for his royal sympathies. His brother Henry (1621-1695) was a famous Welsh scholar of equal merit in both law and medicine. He later became a poet of national standing and in one of his poems he foresaw his eventual burial beside his beloved river, the Usk. In 1655 Henry also wrote the acclaimed poem about the yew, 'The Palm Tree'(see Chapter 3).

The river valley in these parts is full of historical interest, having been a north–south route for millennia. Llanhamlach church has interesting monuments, and a Bronze Age standing stone is situated on floodlands just east of Llansanffraed.

To the south-west lies the Talybont Reservoir, and close by to the north-east is that mystical stretch of water, Llangorse Lake (*Llyn Syfaddan*), which carries many legends attached to the crannogs that once dotted the lake waters. There is a Welsh saying, '*Hyd a llyswen Syfaddan*' – 'as long as a Syfaddan eel', because fish of tremendous size are reputed to inhabit the lake. The partial remains of a rare reliquary were recovered from the lake in the not too distant past (see Detailed Studies – Gwytherin, p. 37).

Overlooking the lake to the south is the hamlet of Cathedin, where the white church of St Michael has three stalwart yews for company. William Condry, writing in 1970, said that they were 'at least one thousand years older than the un-Welsh-looking church'. The middle of the three yews is a male almost 6 metres round.

Llanelli (SO 23231485)

Almost complete circle of yews

Condry's other reference to churchyard yews in these parts is his description of the ring of yews at Llanelli – not to be confused with the large town in Carmarthenshire, although this Breconshire village shares the same sixth-century saint, Elli. The church sits on a hill between the Usk and Clydach. Condry wrote: 'nowhere have I felt more strongly that this was the purpose of churchyard yews - as a magic circle sheltering the dead from the forces of evil'. The yews grow on a low embankment and form an almost complete circle. It would appear that younger trees have been added over the centuries to try to complete the ring. Thirteen of the older trees remain, of which the largest is a female tree of over 6 metres.

Above Llanelli a fine view can be enjoyed looking over the Usk to the mountains beyond. You are now in the limestone country of the Clydach with caves, swallow holes (swirling waters and hidden subterranean passages), and good walking all about.

Llanwenarth Citra (SO 27551481)

Leaning yew

In the south-west corner of the large churchyard of Llanwenarth Citra, located on the narrow flood plain north of the Usk, south of the A40, and west of Abergavenny (*Y Fenni*), there grows a leaning female yew. This tree measures just below 8 metres and is located next to a path behind the church.

Llanfoist (SO 28631320)

Fire-damaged ancient yew

Across the Usk and south-west of Abergavenny the land rises steeply up to the Blorenge (*Y Blorens*), which can be climbed from a woodland path that leads from Llanfoist. The village church at Llanfoist is dedicated to the female saint, Faith, the name probably a corruption of the male Celtic St Ffwyst. In the churchyard the very old 8-metre female yew complements an unusually complete medieval cross. Depicted in a drawing in 1874 the yew has the remains of a wall around its base. In recent times it has suffered either a lightning strike or has been deliberately set on fire, which has given it a 'blasted' appearance. However when last seen (in 2006) it was recovering well from its ordeal.

Mamheilad (SO 30540344)

Five old yews with one of extreme age

Continuing south from Llanfoist and to the west of the A4042 before reaching industrial Pontypool right on the edge of the Brecon Beacons National Park is the hilltop site Mamheilad. Here the church, which overlooks the land to the east, is dedicated to that famous south Welsh saint, Iltyd, and since the 1980s it has had its small church building whitewashed in the old 'style'. If you have only limited time in this area, out of all the sites, Mamheilad is the one to visit. It has five very old yews growing in the raised early medieval enclosure. The oldest and biggest is a truly 'ancient' female yew much measured and discussed in recent times. This tree grows to the right of the path just south of the church porch. It measures over 9 metres, has a 'classic' internal stem, and has been estimated to be over 2000 years old, but more likely its age is commensurate with the early days of the *llan* when the saint set up his 'holy place'. The tree has been recorded as 'ancient' since 1799 and was drawn by the travel writer and illustrator Loudon in 1833.

Capel-y-ffin (SO 25493151)

Five old yews

The final two sites chosen from the Brecon Beacons National Park are a long way apart but have some engaging similarities. They are both found in wild landscapes, neither is on a main route and both have dedications to St Mary. The first is high up in the Black Mountains above Hay-on-Wye at a place called Capel-y-ffin (which translates as 'the boundary chapel'). It marks the place where the river Honddu and the adjacent road enter Monmouthshire from Breconshire. The small quaint church is located south of the Youth Hostel and north of the well-known Llanthony Priory. The church is not particularly old: it was rebuilt in 1762 between two streams that come off the mountainside. The churchyard has eight yews of which seven are of some age; four of these are female. The largest is a fragmentary specimen growing to over 6 metres on the right hand side of the path.

The diarist Reverend Francis Kilvert wrote of the church in the nineteenth century 'squatting like a stout grey owl amongst its seven black yews'. A Benedictine monastery once occupied land near this spot that looks eastwards towards England and the Golden Valley of Herefordshire. The eccentric artist Eric Gill came to live here with his entourage in the 1920s, and the writer Bruce Chatwin received much of his inspiration for his fine novel *On the Black Hill* from the surrounding landscape.

On a lower road across the border in Herefordshire are the ruins of another less well-known abbey site at Craswall. This establishment was run by an order of French monks, the Grandmontaine. Here old yews grow around and out of the decaying monastery walls.

Ystradfellte (SN 93061344)

Several old walled yews

Far over to the west beyond the main ridge of the Beacons in the valley of the Mellte is Ystradfellte (vale of Mellte). This small hamlet can be approached either from the south off the A4059, or from the north over the Roman route *Sarn Helen*, through the wild mountain area of the Fforest Fawr. This is good exploring country where the river Mellte appears and disappears in the limestone caves and gullies.

The churchyard at Ystradfellte is stony and unkempt but in a way that adds to its appeal. The churchyard yews have high rough stone walls around them. The biggest of the trees once had a huge low-spreading limb that has now been severed at about a metre above ground level, and because of this any girth measurement below the cut seems somewhat irrelevant as it gives an exaggeratedly high figure.

Ystradfellte has a special quality and the village and valley are worth the trouble finding. To the north the mountains rise up to over 700 metres before dropping down to the Senni valley and the great yew site at Defynnog. To the east of the mountain road is the great boulder '*Maen Llia*', an indication of early human activity in these parts. There is also a good Latin-inscribed memorial positioned by the old *Sarn Helen* (now a track) on the northern route out of the valley.

Wye Valley and Vale of Usk

Llanddewi Rhydderch (SO 34991296)

One distinctive tall female yew

To the east of Abergavenny and north of the main A40 trunk road, which cuts a swathe through the rolling countryside between the rivers Usk and Trothy (*Troddi*), are two sites with big yews. Closest to Abergavenny and situated on hilly land directly east is Llanddewi Rhydderch. The church's dedication, as the name suggests, is to St David.

The churchyard, located near the Pant brook, is home to a tall, striking-looking 7-metre female yew that includes in her hollow bole a large internal stem, only visible from the church side of the tree. The yew grows only 3 metres from the east side of the church building at the junction of two paths.

Inside the church the altar window has some lovely stained glass; from the churchyard there are fine views towards the Ysgyryd Fawr hill.

Llanarth (SO 37561096)

One very old yew

Heading in a south-easterly direction down winding Monmouthshire lanes from Llanddewi you soon reach St Teilo's church at Llanarth. Here the impressive ancient female yew is well over 9 metres and is located between the gate and the entrance porch east of the path. The yew shows all the characteristics of longevity: it is heavily decayed, has much internal rooting and supports newer growth within its hollow centre.

The nearby St Teilo's Well was once an integral part of the churchyard enclosure before the 'shrinking' of the boundary. The church establishment can be traced back to the sixth century and Llanarth was probably an important monastic centre with much Christian influence in this beautiful area near the Usk.

Goetre (SO 32710592)

Three big yews

The next three sites are close to the river Usk as it heads south towards the town bearing the same name. The first of these is Goetre ('home in the wood'). The parish church of St Peter is located north of what makes up the present settlement, and is east of the main Pontypool road.

In the old churchyard are three big yews: the biggest, a female, grows between the old preaching cross and the porch. On the opposite side of the path is the huge stump of what was an even bigger yew, unfortunately felled over thirty years ago, its hollow core now planted with ornamental creepers. The third of the big yews grows partly within the churchyard wall flanking the road.

Llanfair Kilgeddin (*Llanfair Cilgedin*) (SO 35590869)

Two old yews

Down lanes to the east of Goetre and the B4598, near Pant-y-Goitre Park (good veteran trees here), and positioned in a quiet loop of the river Usk is the redundant church of St Mary at Llanfair Kilgeddin. Like Goetre church it is some way off the main village. This ancient churchyard is bounded on its north, west and east sides by a stream that flows into the Usk. Originally three ancient churchyard yews were recorded here: now only two remain, plus another fairly substantial yew in the corner of the site. The cut-up remains of the third 'ancient' can still (2009) be found stacked beside the farm track just outside the southern bank of the churchyard, presumably too large and difficult to reduce to firewood. The colossal female yew closest to the churchyard cross is well over 8 metres round and has a huge spreading crown.

Of great interest here is the young tree growing some 6 metres away on the west side of the yew. Is this a layered branch from the main yew, or a seedling? If layered, is this an early example of what we now see at Defynnog, and could it add weight to the view that the two female Defynnog yews originate from the same rootstock? Maybe this is an ideal place for an archaeological investigation to take place.

An additional feature of this terrific site is an impressive oak, which overhangs the church gate. Inside the church (key obtainable) are some highly-regarded and stunningly beautiful Victorian wall murals cut into the plastered walls. They were commissioned by an incumbent vicar in memory of his wife Rosamund who died in 1885. The murals were engraved by Heywood Sumner (of Arts and Crafts Society fame) in 1888. The church was fortunately saved from the bulldozer in the 1990s by the Friends of Friendless Churches.

Betws Newydd (SO 36220587)

Several big yews including a decayed giant
Not far away but on the east side of the river is another excellent site in the village of Betws Newydd. The church at Betws Newydd ('new prayer house') is very much in use but is undedicated, although speculation links this site with St Aeddan. There is much of interest here. The remains of a preaching cross are in the churchyard. In the small church there is an impressive rood screen with a rare loft and tympanum, plus a fine Norman font. The name of the village and its location must give this location an early Christian beginning.

The much measured ancient female yew growing north-west of the church was featured in an 1876 drawing in the *Gardeners Chronicle*. The drawing shows the large internal stem, which seems to have changed little over the last century. The internal growth now measures over 2 metres round, and the outer decaying shell is in excess of 10 metres. The tree was estimated at 4,000 years old in the mid 1990s, but although very old seems unlikely to be of that age. Another old yew grows to the east and a younger tree with a smooth straight bole (good for measuring) is near the boundary to the left of the entrance gate.

If time is limited and visits to only a small selection of sites in this area are possible, Betws Newydd and Llanfair Kilgeddin should be near the top of your list!

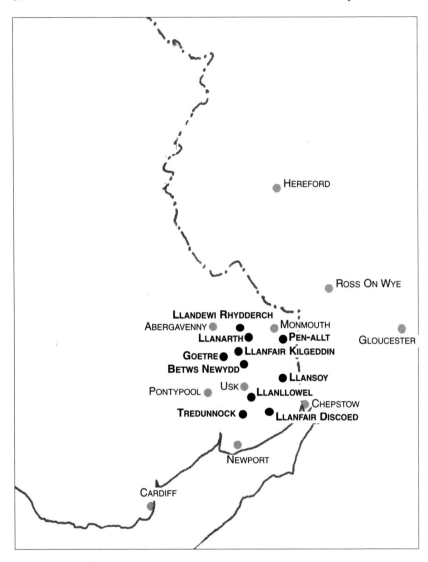

Wye Valley & Vale of Usk

Llansoy (*Llan-soe*) (SO44210239)

Big spreading yew

The major routes leading from the English border to South Wales, and vice versa, divide old Monmouthshire in two, with the east side of the river Usk and the A449 having several good yew sites. One of the most important of these is at Llansoy, originally a monastic site, now a village a few miles east of the town of Usk. The small sloping churchyard is dominated by a huge 8-metre male yew. Several reports in recent years record this tree as having both male and female characteristics, but on a visit in 2006 no female branches were noted.

The history of St Tysoe's church at Llansoy goes back to the eighth century. The present church contains some impressive modern stained glass work.

One of the sadder aspects of yew tree sites in this region is the destruction in recent years of the ancient yews at Llangwm Uchaf and Llangovan (*Llangofen*). Hopefully increased awareness will prevent this occurrence in the future.

Pen-allt (SO 52191073)

Single old yew overlooking deep valley

Further east a short distance from the town of Monmouth in the high wooded country above the River Wye is the settlement of Pen-allt ('pen' translates as 'head' and 'allt' as 'wooded place'). Through narrow lanes with high hedges you eventually reach the 'old' church of St Mary. Here the ridge of Troypark Wood separates you from the town of Monmouth (*Trefynwy*), only one and a half miles away as the crow flies, but it's a long way by road. From the church you can enjoy an inspiring view to the steep woods of Lord's Grove on the English side of the Wye valley. The church has a high square tower and an old sundial over the porch and it is, like many other old churches, a nationally important bat-roost.

The ancient female yew of Pen-allt is to the east of the church and measures over 7 metres. It grows on sloping ground, and from the altar window inside the church you can clearly see the crown of the tree!

The tapestry on the wall near the altar reminds us that Pen-allt was once on the pilgrimage route to Santiago de Compostela in Spain. There is a relatively newly-planted pleached lime avenue between the lych gate and the church door, and very tall older limes adorned with mistletoe grow on the boundary. Just to add to the arboreal scene a very old sweet chestnut is found just outside the churchyard.

Llanllowel (*Llanllywel*) (ST 39269858)

Split tree with metal brace

Moving south down the A449 and back to the banks of the Usk our next site is the village of Llanllowel, with the small Norman church dedicated to St Llywel, a sixth-century companion of St Teilo. It was no doubt once a peaceful place, but now the the busy A449 roars by above it. In the churchyard grows an old, split 7-metre male yew with a limb now secured by a metal brace keeping it away from the church and the path.

There are also two big Irish yews by the entrance gate and a huge alder casts its shade over the small stream at the edge of the churchyard.

Tredunnock (*Tredynog*) (ST 37999485)

Four old yews

Further south again and after crossing the Usk at Newbridge, a popular angling spot, is the village of Tredunnock, with St Andrew's church at its heart. Church history tells us that the original dedication at Tredunnock was probably to the sixth-century St Cybi. The large churchyard is approached through an inner Victorian gate with a 1902 detail, and from the northern boundary wall there are fine views overlooking the fertile Vale of Usk. A beautifully inscribed Roman stone reputedly from the second century AD is displayed inside the church. This 'grave slab' was found buried near the church and is a clear indication of not only the antiquity of the site but also its pre-Christian beginnings.

Three old yews grow in the burial ground with a further tree outside near the lych gate. The largest yew is a squat-looking female tree on the south side of the church. There are also various conifers on the site including a large redwood tree. Limes and horse chestnuts add to the ornamental aspect of the spot.

Llanfair Discoed (*Llanfair Is-coed*) (ST 44639242)

Tall old yew

The last of the featured sites is to the east of Tredunnock and the Forest of Wentwood (Coed Gwent Woodland Trust). The well kept and attractive village of Llanfair Discoed is situated on sloping ground north of the old Roman road near Caerwent. The village is overlooked by the hillfort of Llanmelin. The dedication of the church at Llanfair Discoed is to St Mary. In the small churchyard there is a tall male yew of almost 7 metres round. This tree was noted as a fine specimen by T H Thomas in 1880.

The churchyard looks over the flat landscape that stretches out towards the Roman fort of *Venta Silurum* at Caerwent and further on towards the Severn estuary. On the north-western boundary of the churchyard is the site of the old castle where, over the years, various Roman treasures have been found, and down the lane beyond the village inn the old 'holy well' adds weight to the tradition that Llanfair was indeed a very early Christian place. Inside the church, updated in parts to provide an area for community projects and events, there are some fine examples of both modern and older stained glass.

South-eastern Wales

This region covers Glamorgan and west Monmouthshire where there are a number of good yew sites spread across the land west of Newport (*Casnewydd*) through to the Gower Peninsula near Swansea (*Abertawe*). Although much of the land is now commercial and urban, old churchyards from the pre-industrial past remain as a reminder of the earlier settlements established before the Norman Conquest.

Llanedern (ST 22058199)

Burnt old yew

Llanedern church is north-east of Cardiff city centre and situated by a wayside hostelry on an old road now blocked off by a new arterial highway. It is best reached from either Junction 30 of the M4, or off the A48.

   This enclosure near the Afon Rhymni is from a different age and time, and is now a sort of 'spiritual island' surrounded by all that goes with twenty-first-century edge-of-city living. The big churchyard yew next to the south porch has not avoided malicious intentions, for several times over the past few years it has been 'torched'. The yew, which grows in two distinct pieces, has parts of its crown now dead or dying as a result of the fire damage. Originally the tree would have afforded excellent shelter for the south door, but now that entrance is seldom used and the tree is but a shadow of its former majestic self.

   Externally the church is a rather faded whitewashed affair, but internally it is a picture of loving care and attention. It is built on banked ground, and steps go down into the nave from the tower door. A gentle slope takes you towards the sanctuary. We are told that it was in the sixth century that the local saint Edern first established his *llan* here in south Wales and the church still carries his dedication.

   Down old lanes only a short distance north of Llanedern but north of the M4 is another churchyard yew at Michaelston-y-Fedw (*Llanfihangel-y-fedw*). It grows north of the church, and as at Llanedern there are two separate living pieces.

St Brides-super-Ely (*Llansanffraed-ar-Elái*) (ST 09687762)

Large male yew

To the west of Cardiff and south of the M4 (junction 33), an attractive narrow church stands in the delightfully named St Brides-super-Ely. St Bride is the anglicised name for St Brigid (St Ffraid). The churchyard at St Bride's is home to an excellent ancient male yew, which was once larger than its 7-metre size of today: over the years bits have broken off the trunk, so reducing girth measurement. Even though it is so close to the Cardiff suburbs this sloping churchyard by a stream retains its peaceful early Christian feel.

Pendoylan (*Pendeulwyn*) (ST 05977668)

Twin-stemmed yew

On the opposite side of the Afon Elái and in the fertile Vale of Glamorgan is the church and churchyard of St Cadoc at Pendoylan. The church stands next to the village pub,

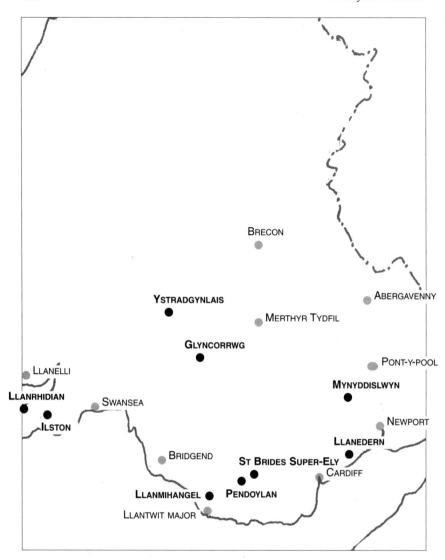

South-eastern Wales

and in the corner of the churchyard between the pub and the church is an ancient male yew. Not unusually it grows on a pronounced mound, and the tree has formed two distinct stems that emanate from a low fork. The yew measures almost 8 metres round and another many-stemmed yew grows to the east on a steep bank at the edge of the churchyard.

On the coast at St Donat's near Llantwit Major (*Llanilltyd Fawr*) there was once a big old churchyard yew depicted in a Victorian painting. It stood near the unusually complete medieval cross, but though the tree has now gone, the cross remains.

Llanmihangel (*Llanfihangel y Bont-faen*) (SS 98137189)
One old yew
Located between Pendoylan and Llantwit Major and south of the A48 on a minor road is the locality of Llanmihangel. The most well-known local feature is the rambling sixteenth-century mansion Plas Llanmihangel, home for many centuries to the well-known local family of Thomas. Many yews are contained within the mansion's period landscaped garden and can be seen at a distance from the nearby road.

On the southerly side is St Michael's church and by the road and churchyard path is St Anne's Well (recently restored). The well was once an elaborate affair with water entering the pool through a sculptured stone figure. That has now disappeared but the existence of the well gives an indication of the antiquity of the site. That is further endorsed by the existence of a large old male yew growing on the south side of the church close to the churchyard boundary.

Somewhat unusually in today's world St Michael's church has no electricity connection: the congregation relies on the old fashioned method of candle illumination!

The Gower peninsula
On the much visited Gower peninsula there are two churchyards worthy of attention for the yew enthusiast. These two sites are an integral part of no fewer than fifteen that make up the Gower churches trail named 'In the Steps of the Saints'. That so many sites exist in this very beautiful but relatively small coastal peninsula is an indication of the importance it must have held in the early medieval period.

Ilston (*Llanilltyd Gŵyr*) (SS 55669034)
Tall female yew
The first of these yew sites is at Ilston, a village close to but far enough away from the Gower coasts and its crowds. The tall, beautifully proportioned female yew cannot be missed, growing as she does within a low wall on a steep mound to the south-east of the church. To reach the churchyard you cross a footbridge over the river Ilston.

If you have time, take the lovely woodland walk following the dingle where in spring the pungent smell of wild garlic perfumes the air and all about is birdsong. You may even catch a sight of a Dipper bobbing on the brook's boulders! The churchyard at Ilston is reputedly the site of a sixth-century monastic cell dedicated to that most famous of early Christians, Illtyd from Llantwit Major.

Llanrhidian (SS 49629223)

Prominent tall yew

Overlooking the wide expanse of the grazed salt marshes on the north side of the Gower is the second site at Llanrhidian. Here the double-dedicated church (SS Illtyd and Rhidian) sits tight to the hillside, and although much altered over the years it has kept its fort-like tower. To reach the church from the main gate you pass two big stones on the village green, one plain and the other supposedly the broken remains of a Celtic cross. Also of great interest is the rough limestone block found years ago hereabouts but now positioned in the porch. Its local name is 'The Leper Stone' and it displays some mysterious carvings of what appear to be human and animal figures.

Llanrhidian's female yew, like that at Ilston, is very prominent as it towers over the gravestones on a steep bank to the south of the church building. Close by is the stump of a long-deceased yew.

A further 'trail church' is right on the coast in woodlands above Oxwich. The church hugs the hillside next to the wide curve of the bay and is reached via a short pleasant walk through the sand dunes from the café and car park. Amongst the many interesting old gravestones grows a multi-stemmed male yew that indicates the site of the well spring of St Illtyd (yet another dedication). The yew is probably older than it appear, as the tree growth seen today is all from an older base. In *The Holy Wells of Wales* Francis Jones makes reference to seven yews growing in a field above Oxwich church and well.

Ystradgynlais (SN 78701007)

One yew

At Ystradgynlais, at the head of the Swansea valley (A4067), just outside the Brecon Beacons National Park, is the church and churchyard of St Cynog where a female yew grows to over 7 metres within a dry stone wall. The present church at Ystradgynlais was constructed on a different alignment to the original church, so the orientation of building to yew has changed over time.

Glyncorrwg (SS 87429930)

Four yews, one twin-stemmed

The only yew site in the region from the western side of the mining valleys is at a small remote village above Maesteg and Cymer (A4107). Long before industrialisation came to south Wales Glyncorrwg had its own early *llan* site. In 1811 there is a record of five yews growing around the church of St John the Baptist. Of those five, four now remain, growing within walls, the largest of which is a twin-stemmed female tree. One of the 'walled' yews is now but a fragment of its 1811 size. Near the porch a large old ash tree grows within a wall and has the look of a 'self set' tree. Positioned as it is by the porch, is it now occupying the space once taken by an 'ancient' yew?

The evocative sound of tumbling water can be heard as the rivulet, the Corrwg, passes below the churchyard wall as it heads for the river Afan. The village, which sits below Craig-y-llyn mountain, has the unenviable reputation of being the wettest village in Glamorgan, and on entering the valley it certainly feels as though you are visiting a long forgotten place! However, when the sun shines the views all around are inspiring. In recent times the growth sport of mountain biking has brought added visitor interest to the forests that cover these hillsides, as have the Afan Forest Park and Visitor Centre, now a hub for trails and walks.

Mynyddislwyn (ST 19349391)

Six old yews – five in a line on hilltop site
The remaining featured yew site from the industrial region of south Wales lies on the eastern side, on an old mountain road above Risca. Mynyddislwyn is situated on high terrain west of Newbridge and best accessed off the A472 near Pontllan-fraith. Once you climb off the main road you are transported back to an older landscape of hedgerows, battered lines of veteran beeches, and the remnant estate lands that once covered these hillsides.

At Mynyddislwyn the present hilltop church of St Tudor (1820) has an odd 'castle style' tower, and is located next to an inn. Although the church building is a relatively recent structure, the site reputedly dates back to the sixth century. It has benefited from Heritage Lottery funding, and newly-laid flagstone paths take you toward the church and yew trees. The churchyard is home to six walled yews with five of them growing in a line. A further empty square wall probably once held another yew. The biggest is a male tree growing from three distinct stems. A tumulus rising next to the churchyard is appropriately named Twyn Tudur ('Tudor's mound') and has many superstitions and legends connected to it, although its true significance remains a mystery.

A famous local man of the parish was Benjamin Hall, who had the distinction of having the bell in the famous clock tower outside the Houses of Parliament in London named after him – 'Big Ben'.

For a exciting way back to the 'modern world' drive carefully down the lane beside Twyn Tudor. It drops steeply by woodland and fields to come out by a bridge near Wattsville and the Sirhowy Valley Country Park.

South-western Wales

This region consists of the old counties of Carmarthenshire, Ceredigion, and the peninsular county of Pembrokeshire. The latter, alas, has now only one surviving ancient yew within its boundaries. Carmarthenshire is traditionally sheep country, but during the twentieth century became noted more as 'conifer country', especially on her upland areas.

Ystrad-ffin (SN 78764704)

Large yew near porch

At the county's heart is the long and narrow Brianne Reservoir and around it are several picturesque river valleys, the most well known being the Tywi.

South of the reservoir near the conical Dinas hill is a remote chapel with a seven-metre male yew. This hollow tree grows near the porch of St Paulinus' chapel at the location of Ystrad-ffin. The first recorded chapel here dates from 1112 and in recent centuries it has been supported by the landowners, the Cawdor family.

This area is full of interest including, on the western flank of Dinas hill, the cave of Twm Shôn Cati, a sixteenth-century romantic bandit figure. Dinas is now an RSPB reserve and the car park servicing the hill abuts the churchyard (park here). A mile away there is also the nature reserve at Doethie. It was around this area that the very small residual Welsh population of Red Kites struggled to keep hold during the twentieth century before their re-expansion in recent years.

Cil-y-cwm (SN 75334002)

Five yews

Following the Tywi south but crossing the river at Rhandirmwyn (note a huge oak by the roadside) and before reaching the town of Llandovery (*Llanymddyfri*) you reach Cil-y-cwm, where the fourteenth-century church of St Michael has five yews growing around it. The largest of these trees is a striking-looking male with a smooth light-coloured, almost bleached, trunk. It grows at the far end of the narrow churchyard close to both the church's south-east corner and a whitewashed building.

After reaching Llandovery you now follow the Tywi in a westerly direction as it broadens out into a fertile valley. The busy A40 now becomes the river's companion as it passes Llandeilo. St Teilo's church has much to offer those interested in early Celtic Christian sites, for displayed inside are inscribed stones and a 'state of the art' early medieval manuscript exhibition, both of which are well worth seeing. On the western fringe of the town is the National Trust's Dinefwr Park, historic home of the Rhys family, with its herd of distinctive White Park cattle. Here are excellent walks, a ruined castle and many veteran parkland trees.

Llangathen (SN 58442214)

Several big yews

Further down the valley and between the main road (A40) and the northern banks of the Tywi is Llangathen. From a small hilltop the thirteenth-century church of St Cathen looks out over the river meadows. The most distinctive external feature of the church is its tall Edwardian-style 'military' tower. Of Llangathen's churchyard yews the most impressive is a male tree growing at the junction of two footpaths directly in front of main gate. The bole of the yew is enclosed in a high double wall. Recent tree maintenance work has included ivy removal and some light pruning.

Displayed inside the church are a fine Tudor table and a monument to John Dyer, the celebrated Anglo-Welsh poet (1699-1758), who lived nearby at Aberglasney Mansion. At the time of the ambitious restoration of the overgrown gardens at Aberglasney in the 1990s, what later became referred to as the 'yew tunnel' was revealed. This feature turned out to be a neglected path flanked by 'trained' yews that had 'fused' together to form an archway. Later research told us that the yews formed part of the original eighteenth-century landscape design. The 'tunnel' shows to good effect the extraordinary coalescing characteristics of yew branches when growing in close proximity to one another. John Dyer wrote some notable poems about the area including an evocative description of the nearby hill-fort Grongar Hill – 'Ever charming ever new, When will the landscape tire the view!' The extraordinary Dyer spent some time as an itinerant artist, and one his greatest poems 'The Fleece' concerned the working lives of eighteenth-century Welsh shepherds, among whom he lived for a while.

Llandybïe (SN 61831555)

Much-pruned yew

South of the Tywi and Llangathen but before reaching Ammanford (A483) you come to the expanded village of Llandybïe, which has to its east the Black Mountain and the whole of the Brecon Beacon National Park. The church here is dedicated to the fifth-century saint Tybie, and in the churchyard to the right of the lych gate is a stumpy old female yew encircled by a rough dry stone wall. The crown of the tree has been reduced over time (mainly to avoid the overhead service wires) to leave the squat wide top seen today. Only the sizeable trunk indicates the antiquity of the yew.

The church has several unusual whitewashed arches down the centre of its nave and also has a military tower similar to that at Llangathen. It contains a bust of the poet Henry Vaughan of Derwydd. At the north end of the village a steep lane west leads through Pentregwenlais and a much disturbed old quarried landscape. Keep left, and on the north side of the lane, where a track goes off to Carreggwenlais Farm, is the wellspring *Ffynnon Gwenlais,* from which a small rivulet eminates. Water erosion of the underlying limestone has resulted in the local map being dotted with caves and springs. Above the walled well a 500-year old yew marks the head of the stream, first recorded in the late seventeenth century when the Welsh topographical writer Edward Lhyud toured this area. He also recorded seeing a chapel here. The yew and spring are on private land but can be observed fairly closely from the quiet roadside pull-in that is on higher ground above the stream.

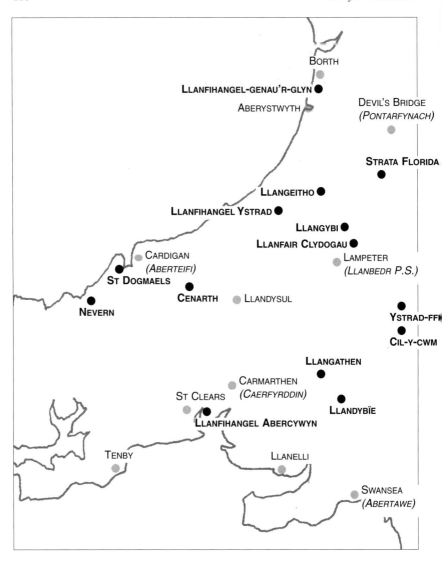

South-western Wales

Llanfihangel Abercywyn (SN 30201330)

Male yew near ruins

At the county town of Carmarthen (*Caerfyrddin*) the Afon Tywi heads south towards Carmarthen Bay, where it meets the tidal mouth of the Carmarthenshire Taf. Flowing into the Taf, after coming through some wooded dingles a few miles north, is the small river, the Afon Cywyn, which ends with a meander along a marshy level before meeting the salt water of the Taf.

On either side of the Cywyn are two old ruined churches that almost face each other across the waters; both take their name from the river. On the west side is the church of St Michael at Llanfihangel Abercywyn. The roofless ruin stands alone on the sloping fields that gently fall away towards the reed-banked tideline of the Taf. The remains have amongst their arboreal companions a fine old female yew growing close by the walls. Below this tree and some neighbouring conifers are some so-called 'pilgrim graves': it is thought, however, they are more likely to be the graves of local folk who built the church in the twelfth century. Whoever they were, their graves could hardly be in a quieter or more peaceful spot with just the wind and the sounds of the wildfowl for company. Now not even a track leads down to the old church site. To reach it you travel by foot on private land past the farmhouse and large farmyard named Trefenty. You then make your way across the low fields to this atmospheric place by the rivers.

On the east side is Llandeilo Abercywyn (St. Teilo's church at the mouth of the Cwywn) and also a stopping place for the medieval pilgrims heading for St David's. The history of the church is confirmed in the English name of the adjacent farmhouse: 'Pilgrim's Rest'.

Cenarth (SN 27034150)

Fragments of male yew

On the north-west borders of Carmarthenshire that most inspiring of rivers, the Teifi, makes its way down from the north. At first the river flows gently then after Newcastle Emlyn (*Castell Newydd Emlyn*) it begins its rush towards the sea at Cardigan (*Aberteifi*). Amongst the villages it passes is Cenarth, famed for its coracles, salmon fishing and riverside inns. More recently it has acquired museums, tea and souvenir shops and car parks – all there to cater for the many summer visitors that pass this way. To see the river at its most dramatic, though, it is best to visit when the waters are in spate as they tumble at speed over the smooth rocks and through the deep pools.

On the southern side of the river, uphill from the elegant eighteenth-century road bridge (A484), is the easily missed church of St Llawddog, with its raised churchyard. On the southern side of the church porch is the old male yew of Cenarth. All that is left of this veteran are three fragments (one fallen) that spread the crown wide apart. There are also various props and straps placed there to keep the tree together, and only recently a limb collapsed to the ground – thankfully still growing from the living tissues of the main tree. The base of the tree is contained within a wall originally built in the eighteenth century.

Other indications of early Christian activity in the area are demonstrated by the impressive inscribed stone known as the 'Gellidywyll Stone' positioned in the churchyard near the slope down to the road. This stone was apparently moved from a nearby field at Parc Maen Llwyd in the early part of the twentieth century. The saint's holy well at Cenarth is encased in a small restored structure south-west of the road bridge by the salmon pools.

St. Dogmaels (*Llandudoch*) (SN 16354585)

Ancient female yew

The river valley continues to Cardigan (*Aberteifi*), where the next site is located on the west side of the Teifi estuary and approached off the B4546 Poppit Sands road. St Dogmaels is home to the remains of a Benedictine Priory. The ruins are sparse but the outlines of the buildings are still recognisable. The far older early medieval church site of St Mary (re-dedication) is in the corner of the priory grounds. Like other medieval orders, the Benedictines had the good sense to set up home on an already sacred site many centuries after the first Christian presence. Displayed within the church is a first class ogham-Latin inscribed stone that was moved from outside (for protection) many years ago. It was this very stone that was used in unravelling the 'mysteries' of ogham inscriptions. Unmissable, for it grows right beside the church porch, are the impressive remains of an ancient female yew, now enclosed in a high circular wall and kept together by steel bands. Will the heavily pruned dark green mass one day 'break out' from its walled enclosure? The rather sanitised-looking Norman ruins are brought to life by this great tree, which was probably growing when the black-robed monks walked the cloisters! St Dogmaels is just in Pembrokeshire, and it now has the distinction of being home to the only known surviving ancient yew in the county. The priory remained in the county only because the lordships of Cemmaes doggedly hung onto ownership rather than allow the Ceredigion lords to occupy all lands around the strategically important Teifi estuary.

For those visiting, it is worthwhile taking time to look at the still-working water-mill wheel and shop located next to the priory site.

At Bridell churchyard, next to the A478 and a short distance from Cardigan, can be found the remaining stumps of several giant yews, recorded in the early twentieth century before they were felled (no record of when). They are near the ogham-inscribed stone to the south of the present church. How many other ancient yews have suffered a similar fate?

Nevern (*Nyfer*) (SN 08334002)

Avenue of eight yews

Between Fishguard (*Abergwaun*) and Cardigan (*Aberteifi*) and located off a minor road (B4582) is the famous churchyard of Nevern. The church is dedicated to the sixth-century St Brynach, a contemporary of St David. Bordering the churchyard, the Caman stream flows on to join the Afon Nyfer below the church. Within and around the church are several very important early Christian monuments. These include the *Maglocunus*

Stone (ogham/Latin), now incorporated into an interior windowsill; the Cross Stone; the *Vitalianus* Stone (ogham/Latin); and the Great Cross, a tall and magnificently inscribed monument located outside the church. There was also a slab stone that had the Greek chi-rho inscription (shown in a sketch in 1861), now sadly gone. You would expect an ancient yew here to complement the stones but none now exists.

There is, however, an impressive but gloomy avenue of eight yews lining the path between the gate and the south porch. The tree known as the 'bleeding yew of Nevern' is the second of these trees on the right (from the gate). The yew is so named due to the crimson-coloured cut branch that was 'sawed' during Victorian tree surgery activities. The branch wound continually exudes a red sticky resin that runs down and stains the trunk. This 'natural' phenomenon (see Bronllys in Brecon region) was originally interpreted as having an association with the Crucifixion and became an added attraction at Nevern, along with the early Christian stones. A line of younger yews marks the southern boundary.

As if the above were not enough, there is a surviving mounting block by the gate, and up the lane by the church are a number of crosses cut into a rock face. This was the site of a medieval wayside shrine, as Nevern was an important pilgrim stop on the route to and from St David's.

Llanfihangel Ystrad (SN 52455622)

Huge female yew

In the heart of Ceredigion there are four sites clustered around an area north of Lampeter (*Llanbedr Pont Steffan*). The first of these is a churchyard located at the point where the Afon Aeron turns north-west towards its meeting with the sea at Aberaeron. Llanfihangel Ystrad (also known as Ystrad Aeron) has a huge female yew growing to the left of the church path leading in from the lych gate. The immense base of this tree has a number of stems growing out of it that have been severely cut back in past decades. The spreading crown covers a wide area. Further along the path, also on the left, is another big female yew. The main door of St Michael's church is away from the road (A482) on the western side.

A minor road to Llanarth and the village of New Quay leads off south-west of the churchyard and the A482.

Llangeitho (SN 62056009)

Several old yews

Towards the head of the broad valley of the Aeron and to the west of the great Roman road Sarn Helen is the village of Llangeitho (B4342). Here the heavily restored church, dedicated to St Ceitho, stands off a lane north of the village centre. Four yews were recorded by John Lowe in 1897, and of these four the largest-girthed tree is a male growing to the west of the church building.

Llangeitho is renowned as the principal preaching place of Daniel Rowland (1713-90), that most fiery of Methodists, whose statue stands next to the chapel in the village. Ironically his father was the Rector of St Ceitho's church.

Llangybi (SN 60865318)

Leaning yew

Two routes travel either side of the river Teifi between Lampeter and Tregaron. Each road has an ancient churchyard and yew. Llangybi is north of Lampeter on the straightened A485 that now by-passes the old bridge and the church of St Cybi. The raised churchyard has a walled embankment around it with a big, rough boulder on the field side to the west. This was possibly a standing stone that was moved to its present position some centuries ago. The unmeasurable female yew leans almost to the ground at the southern end of the churchyard mound, and it now obliterates some old slab gravestones. Despite the structural weakness of the tree it displays a healthy crown.

On the same side of the road 400 metres south of the church is the sympathetically restored St Cybi's well (*Ffynnon Gybi*). The way to the crystal-clear spring is indicated by a finger post. The well is located across the road from the Maesyffynnon Chapel. In the late seventeenth century Lhuyd described the well and the customs associated with it.

Llanfair Clydogau (SN 62445124)

One huge female yew

From Llangybi it is but a short distance down a lane and across a fine old bridge into Llanfair Clydogau (B4343), where three streams come down from the hills to meet the Afon Teifi. Over to the south-west runs *Sarn Helen* as it links with both Ffarmers and Pumsaint and the goldmines at Dolaucothi. To the east of St Mary's church at Clydogau is a huge spreading female yew growing within a wall. Across the road in the corner of a farmyard is a very old gnarled oak tree, but even this veteran cannot match the antiquity of the churchyard yew.

Strata Florida (*Ystrad Fflur*) (SN 74606580)

Two old yews remain from the original thirty-nine recorded in the sixteenth century

Along similar lines to St Dogmaels (see p. 110), where the old churchyard is attached to abbey ruins, Strata Florida (*Ystrad Fflur* – 'vale of flowers') has St Mary's church and churchyard adjacent to its romantic abbey site. Strata Florida, though, was Cistercian, not Benedictine, and there may be two ancient yews, not one. The beautifully situated abbey is found beside the infant river Teifi, east of Pontrhydfendigaid and the Cors Caron National Nature Reserve (B4342). It seems perfectly reasonable to suggest, as Robert Bevan-Jones does in his book The Ancient Yew, that the old churchyard of St Mary pre-dates the twelfth century abbey ruins by some centuries. Evidence is supplied by the discovery of at least one early pre-Norman stone that is now positioned behind the east end of the church building.

In 1539 the topographer Leland recorded no fewer than thirty-nine yews in this extremely large churchyard - the only reference to yews in Leland's entire travel writing. Depicted in a *Gardeners Chronicle* illustration in 1874 is a very old split yew with a 'path' going in between the remaining pieces of the tree. This yew no longer exists, and of Leland's thirty-nine just two survive, a male and female. Greatest attention has been afforded the female tree, as it has long been assumed that this was the tree under which the fourteenth-century poet Dafydd ap Gwilym was buried. This view has been endorsed by the erection of a wall and the placing of a rough memorial below the tree. George Borrow, the travel writer described visiting the grave in 1854. However, after analysing Borrow's account and studying the poem on the burial by Gruffydd Gryg (a contemporary of Dafydd ap Gwilym), Bevan-Jones forcibly argues that the true 'poet's tree' is the male yew that grows by the wall to the north-west, some 60 metres from the female. The male is now only a fragment of its former size, and the female tree is presently recovering from the effects of storm damage and severe restorative tree surgery work early this century.

If visiting Strata Florida and the Cistercian ruins it is recommended that you view the photograph of the storm-damaged tree in the church, then view both yews to observe the decay and re-growth before making your own mind up as to which is the true 'poet's tree'.

Llanfihangel Genau'r-glyn (SN 62328690)

Fragment of very old yew

A Ceredigion church with a St Michael dedication is located north of Aberystwyth on the west side of the B4353 Borth road. The old part of the village of Llandre is named Llanfihangel Genau'r-glyn and is easily missed, as it is reached off a lane that crosses the rural railway line. The mounded churchyard is below a wooded hill, and the old graves are set in terraces amongst the trees on the hillside – the digging could not have been easy! All indications at St Michael's are that it was an early Christian establishment.

The yew drawings by Edwin Lees printed in the *Gardeners Chronicle* of 1874 include one entitled 'Old yew - divided into four boles, near Borth, Cardingshire [*sic*]'. That depiction turned out to be the Llandre female yew, a tree of great age and now consisting of only three, not four 'boles' that grow out of the old rotting core of the original trunk. The earth is very noticeably raised around the base, probably caused by both grave-diggings and the decaying heartwood of the tree. The yew is positioned behind the church and in recent years has had a 'tidy up'. Now an information board is placed rather incongruously in front of the veteran yew.

You can sit here and imagine an early Celtic saint sitting in the same spot contemplating the wonders of creation while looking out over the lower-lying land to the hills and mountains beyond. This picture is enhanced by the existence of a holy well close by the east wall of the churchyard. In the early twentieth century a small building (now gone) stood next to the well, and claims of miracles were recorded from this period. The well and its surroundings have been refurbished and provide a pleasant place to sit.

Llandre is worth a visit not only for its outstanding yew and well site but also for its close proximity to the unspoilt beach at Borth where at very low tide, or after storm conditions, the remains of an ancient submerged forest can be seen. There are good cliff walks, and the nature reserves at Ynyslas, Borth bog and Ynys-hir (RSPB) are close.

Afterword

Although some enclosures now used as churchyards were used for ritual practices as far back as the Bronze Age, that does not necessarily prove that any existing ancient yews date back to that time. It seems more likely that the ancient churchyard yews seen growing today were deliberately planted in those enclosures in the early medieval period. The lack of ancient yews growing on un-Christianised sites supports this view.

Literary sources, particularly from Ireland, point to trees playing an important part in both the pagan and the early Christian conversion period in the Celtic lands. There are a number of biblical references to trees that would have been readily available to influence the scholars of the early Celtic church. It is known that the yew was one of number of tree species holding special significance, as proven by early Welsh and Irish law books. In Wales this is demonstrated by the higher value placed on a consecrated or saint's yew than on a secular one. From out of the pagan past certain individual specimens were deemed to hold protective powers – so much so that in the very beginnings of Christianity in the west some ecclesiastical sites may well have been located near these special trees. That does not mean that wherever there is an ancient yew the site and tree pre-date Christianity: it is much more the case that the tradition of special trees was carried through and used in the early Christian period. The tale in the *Book of Llandaf* that describes the yew at the unidentified site of Miluc raises questions about consecrated or 'holy' ground and the part the yew played within it. For example, was the yew an integral diagnostic feature of the churchyard holy space? The tale tells of Iestyn's men taking away the maiden who had sought protection between the yew tree and the church. This suggests that the yew held a special protective position within the churchyard enclosure. The punishment given out to Iestyn and his criminals was not for violation of the maiden but for violation of the protected space.

When church development progressed in Wales in the early medieval period, special trees were planted within the sacred space that was the churchyard enclosure. Instead of the church going to the tree, the tree went to the church.

Although there are still many unanswered questions regarding the development of the Welsh church during the early medieval period, certain criteria can be used to indicate early church sites. These indicators include church dedications, shape and size of enclosure, in situ inscribed stones, saint's relics, wells and associated legends. Using the list of the oldest known churchyard yews in Wales there appears to be a correlation between the oldest trees and the oldest sites, suggesting deliberate planting at or around the time of the original *llan* establishment.

Questions remain. Did every site have its own 'saint's yew'? And is what we now see just the remnant population of fewer than fifty of the original trees, these having been supplemented by additional plantings over the succeeding centuries? Does the absence of ancient yews from Anglesey and Pembrokeshire tell us that it was only where the species occurred locally that it became planted in churchyards, or were there yews in these counties that were lost for other reasons?

As the churchyard archaeology of Wales develops, the role and age of the old yews may become somewhat clearer. Even so, the problems posed in the measuring of old yews, the unusual and chaotic growth pattern, the absence of the oldest wood to carbon date, and the lack of a tree-ring sequence all contribute to the difficulties of arriving at an accurate age for the oldest trees. Authenticated planting dates and a range of measurements on smooth-boled younger trees can give fairly reliable growth rates, but the ages of the oldest trees can only be estimates.

Assuming then that the oldest trees are up to 1400 years old, the remaining yews have been planted at different periods for a variety of reasons, stimulated by such differing impulses as liturgical use, protection, archery needs and as an indicator of an ecclesiastical site. Over time the yews became part of the 'furniture' of the churchyard, acting as a physical shelter, particularly at times of burial. In fact their function could be seen to be similar to that of the porch or lych gate and could explain the existence of some yews located alongside footpath alignments near churches. Where this occurs, the dark green foliage of the evergreen yew also acted as a 'marker' in the landscape. This could also explain the boundary planting of yews around many churchyards. As well as these utilitarian uses, the green foliage, so prized before the introduction of other evergreen species, was used in ritual funerary and burial practices. This gives added potency and symbolism to the yew in churchyard history.

When referring to ancient yews in English churchyards, the similaries in the appearance of some of the oldest specimens to Welsh trees can be somewhat explained by reading some of the latest studies on church development in pre-Norman England. The available evidence suggests that in seventh- and eighth-century England, local cult sites existed that were similar to those in Wales at the same period. The perceived contrasts between England and the Celtic areas is probably a reflection on the differences in the steady recording over time of minor cults, rather than in actual differences on the ground. During the Norman period churchyard yews continued to be planted, and throughout the Middle Ages there is documentary evidence to show this continuity. This culminated in a 'rash' of Victorian plantings by both parish churches and Nonconformist chapels. These later plantings are not necessarily associated with any form of 'sacred' element.

The lack of more historical literature surrounding the yew in Wales could be due to an 'edginess' within the established church in being associated with idolatrous items such as trees. For example, there does not appear to be any depiction of the yew in Welsh church art. However, the many gaps in the recording of the ecclesiastical history of Wales make the limited references to the yew hardly surprising.

Although some questions may never be fully answered, the fact that today we can see some yews that date from pre-Conquest times should encourage us to value them alongside other early churchyard features – even more so when we consider that both on a practical and a cultural level the yew has been an integral part of Welsh history for more than a millennium. In viewing these places the visitor is not only looking at ancient yews but is also being drawn into the rich history of the site and of the area as a whole.

APPENDIX 1

Notable yews in Wales

Girth measurements are generally taken at 1.5 metres above the highest point of the surrounding ground, or, with a tapering tree, the narrowest point below that point. As referred to previously, measuring the girth of yews, particularly old ones, is often difficult and prone to imprecision, so measurements should only be used as a guide to the antiquity of the tree. On some yews it may be only possible to measure at ground level, or just above. Where measurements have been taken at these points it has been noted in the table in Appendix 1, and all records have been rounded to the nearest 5 centimetres. It is also important to point out that on some extremely old yews the rotting process has left only fragmentary remains. This throws up the possibility that the largest trees may not necessarily be the oldest. Only by more detailed work can a meaningful analysis of these trees and their numbers be arrived at. Nevertheless, as far as present research goes these lists show the position as at 2006.

Sometimes it is worth looking closely at the ground around the main bole, for it is occasionally possible to find old pieces of original or secondary trunks, eg. Llanwrin, Machynlleth, Llantysilio. There are sites where yews grow so close together that they may be from the same rootstock. If this is the case they may be far older than they appear, eg. Merthyr Cynog, Defynnog (more work is required to investigate these trees).

The archaeological classifications of the churchyard sites have been obtained from the four Welsh archeological trusts: Clwyd-Powys (CPAT), Cambria Archaeology (Dyfed Archaeological Trust), Glamorgan-Gwent, and Gwynedd. Each trust has a different method of classification, so no common assessment method is possible at present.

The Glamorgan-Gwent Trust has graded church sites of possibly pre-Norman origin from A to D. Grade A denotes certain pre-Norman origin, Grade B probable, Grade C/D possible.

Cambria Archaeology and the Gwynedd Trust supply a list of likely early medieval sites for their regions. The system employed by CPAT for the Welsh Historic Churches Project has been used in the following table. Of the forty-two sites with 8-metre girthed yews only four are considered as being from a period after the Norman Conquest. All of the nineteen sites with 9-metre-girthed yews only two sites are classified as from the medieval period. One of those churchyards, Disgoed, is now likely to be re-classified as pre-Norman. It seems therefore reasonable to suggest that the biggest yews could be used alongside notable archaeological features as an additional indicator of the antiquity of a site.

The list of historic Welsh churches, produced in *Church Archaeology* in 2000, revealed 943 churches founded before 1800. Of these forty-two have yews that have girths exceeding 8 metres, which equates to 4.5 per cent of all sites. None of these trees are located outside of the church list, none are found in the historic counties of

Anglesey, Flintshire and Pembrokeshire, and only one in Glamorgan. It is interesting to note that in both Anglesey and Pembrokeshire the yew is absent from the flora records, so suggesting that the occurrence of ancient churchyard yews has a direct relationship with where the species is found in the local landscape. However, it is also worth noting that a site visit to Pembrokshire in March 2006 revealed the burnt remains of a very large yew near the well known inscribed ogham stone in Bridell churchyard. This yew had been approximately 9 metres in girth at ground level and very hollow. In October 1870 R. R. Brash visited the churchyard to inspect the pillar stone and he reported in *Archaeologia Cambrensis* that the graveyard was small, and overgrown with trees, amongst which were some yews of great age and size: 'Under one of these stood the fine ogham pillar-stone shewn in the illustration, at the south side of the church'. A relatively young yew now growing close to the path and churchyard monuments gives the appearance of being a seedling from one of the original yews on this site. At nearby St Dogmaels (*Llandudoch*) an old yew grows within a high wall near the doorway of the present church, in which is located an early inscribed stone found some years ago on the site. Both Bridell and St Dogmaels are located in the extreme north-east of Pembrokeshire.

It is worth emphasising two points. Firstly, there are yews that are close to the 8 metre mark that are not listed, as a cut-off point was required for this exercise. Secondly, a more refined list of early medieval church sites incorporating the old yews would not only raise the percentage dramatically, but would also produce a more relevant comparison. Unfortunately such a refined list is not available in a common format at present.

It is possible that at least one yew was planted as an integral feature of the churchyard on every pre-Norman ecclesiastical site where the yew could be found growing locally. Over time many of these original trees were lost and what is left is the relic population, added to by new plantings right up to the present day: for example, the many yews planted during the millennium celebrations of AD 2000.

Some historical Welsh yew measurements

In the following paragraphs are some historical records taken from a variety of sources on various Welsh churchyard yews.

The yew now growing behind a tall iron railing in Gresford churchyard, near Wrexham was first recorded in 1813, again in 1836 and also in 1878 by Sir Robert Christison. In 1897 John Lowe looked at the various measurements taken on the Gresford yew during the nineteenth century and highlighted the differences in the apparent rates of growth of various parts of the tree. He concluded, 'how very fallacious this mode of estimating age is'.

The churchyard yew at Llanddewi Fach, near Caerleon, was first recorded by J. G. Strutt in 1822 as possessing an internal stem. T H Thomas not only referred to the tree as a notable specimen but in 1880 produced a detailed water colour of it. John Lowe had the tree measured as 30 feet 4 inches at 3 feet above ground level in 1897. Lowe described the tree as having a stunted hollow trunk with a lateral opening that 'will hold five or six persons'. He makes reference to the internal stem taking over the growth of the tree. According to Allen Meredith the tree was cut down and burnt in 1975.

Of historical interest is Archdeacon Coxe's report of finding the largest yew growing in St Illtyd's churchyard at Mamheilad near Pontypool, in 1799. He was sufficiently interested in the tree to measure its girth at 25 feet. A sketch of the tree was made by J C Loudon in 1833. It shows the enormous internal growth observed later by Strutt and Lowe (clearly evident in the spring of 2006). Some sixty years later, in 1895, the yew was measured by Rev. Cook for John Lowe. In 1929 H A Hyde measured the Mamheilad yew, which he named the 'Queen of Yews', at 30 feet 4 inches from ground level. Hyde listed twenty-one other Welsh yews with girths exceeding 20 feet. In 1972 the tree recorder Alan Mitchell listed the largest-girthed yews he had measured during the period 1958 to 1970 and he only included one Welsh tree, the Mamheilad yew.

The yew trees of Guilsfield (*Cegidfa*) churchyard near Welshpool (*Trallwng*) were documented in 1888 and according to records a 'J Jones' held a document showing that twelve of the yews were planted in the reign of William and Mary and were therefore all of a similar age. A female yew, not one of those twelve and growing close to the churchyard's right hand gatepost (looking out from the porch), has an interesting history. On the curious raised tomb is the following inscription 'Under this yew tree, Buried would hee bee, For his father and he Planted this yew tree'. Details contained within the church tell the story of a man of ninety being buried in his father's grave below the yew, which was planted in approximately 1625. If this is correct it gives a valuable insight into growth rates of yews. The tree has a smooth bole, good for measuring, and in September 2005 it measured 3 metres and 65 centimetres (12 feet) girth. The yew then has grown at an average of half a centimetre circumference for each year of its 380 years.

The list below includes all known churchyard yews in Wales with girth measurements exceeding 8 metres. Measurements are taken at the narrowest point below 1.5 metres unless indicated.

Measures referred to in the text are metric girth/circumference.

F = female, M = male, + = greater than, ag = at ground, DS = Detailed Study

Place	Dedication	Measurement cms	sex	Features	Churchyard Classification
Alltmawr	St Mauritius	840	M		Poss pre N
Betws Newydd*	Poss. Aeddan	1000	F		Poss pre N
Betws Penpont	undedicated	810	M		Post med
Buttington	All Saints	820	M		Med
Cenarth	St Llawddog	850	M	Well, in/d stone	Pre N
Cregrina	St David	800 ag	M		Med
Cyffylliog	St Mary	890	F		Med
Defynnog* (DS)	St Cynog	1130 ag	F	Inscribed stone	Pre N (clasau)
		850	F		
Discoed*	St Michael	900+	M	Well	Poss pre N
Gresford (*Gresffordd*)	All Saints	890	M	Inscribed stone	Poss pre N
Gwytherin (DS)	St Winifred	830	F	Inscribed stones	Pre N
		820	F		
Llanafan Fawr*	St Afan	970 ag	F	Pre N insc.	Pre N (clasau)
Llanarth*	St Teilo	990 ag	M	Well nearby	Pre N
Llanddeiniolen*	St Deiniolen	880	M	Well nearby	Poss pre N
		950	F		
Llandeilo Graban	St Teilo	800 ag	M		Poss pre N
Llandrillo-yn-Edeirnion*	St Trillo	Split (unmeasurable)	F	Well nearby	Pre N
Llanedern	St Edeyrn	820	F		Poss pre N
Llanelltyd*	St Illtyd	900	F		Poss pre N
Llanerfyl* (DS)	St Erfyl	Split (unmeasurable)	F	Stone & shrine	Pre N
Llanfair Kilgeddin (*Llanfair Cilgedin*)	St Mary	830	F		Poss pre N
		830 ag	F		
Llanfaredd*	St Mary	910	F	Well nearby	Poss pre N
Llanfeugan*	St Meugan	920 ag	M		Pre N

| Place | Dedication | Measurement | | Features | Churchyard |
		cms	sex		Classification
Llanfihangel Genau'r-glyn*	St Michael	1060 ag	F	Holy well	Pre N
Llanfihangel Nant Melan	St Michael	800 ag	M		Poss pre N
Llanfihangel Ystrad	St Michael	850+	F		Poss pre N
Llanfoist (*Llan-ffwyst*)	St Faith	800 ag	F	19th C drawing	Poss pre N
Llangernyw* (**DS**)	St Digain	1020	M	Insc. stones/ Well	Pre N
Llangwm*	St Jerome	900+	F		Poss pre N
Llansantffraed in Elvel (*Llansantffraed-yn-Elfael*)	St Brigid	800 ag	M	Site of Nunnery	Pre N
Llansilin	St Silin	800	M		Pre N
		800	M		(clasau)
Llansoy (*Llan-soe*)	St Tysoi	870	M		Pre N
Llanspyddid (*Llansbyddyd*)	St Cattwg	880	F	Inscribed Stone	Pre N
Llanwrin*	St Gwrin	900+	M		Pre N
Llanymawddwy	St Tydecho	850 ag	F		Pre N
Machynlleth*	St Peter	900+	M		Poss pre N
Mallwyd*	St Tydecho	1010	M		Poss pre N
Mamheilad*	St Illtyd	950 ag	F		Poss pre N
Nantmel	St Cynllo	850	F		Pre N
Penegoes*	St Cadfarch	900+	M	Well nearby	Poss pre N
Pennant Melangell (**DS**)	St Melangell	870	F	Shrine	Pre N
Rhulen (*Rhiwlen*)	St David	800 ag	M		Pre N
Ystradfellte*	St Mary	1040 ag	M		Poss pre N

* Denotes churchyards with yews exceeding 9 meters in girth (20 in total). Of the forty-two sites on the above list, the classifications are as follows (churchyard classifications via the various archaeological trusts - see p. 116):

19 pre Norman　　　　　　　　19 possibly pre-Norman
3 Medieval　　　　　　　　　　1 post-Medieval

APPENDIX 2
Travelogue

All measurements are for guidance only and where possible are taken at the narrowest point. On some trees measurements can only be taken at ground level (see chapter on measuring yews).

Measures referred to in the text are metric girth/circumference.

f = female, m = male, + = greater than, ag = at ground, un = unmeasurable

Snowdonia and north-west Wales

Site	Dedication	Map Guide	Girth in centimetres	Site Notes
Caerhun	St Mary	SH 77687040	625+ f SW Many Yews	Roman aux. fort *Canovium*. Church in N .E. corner of fort.
Llanddeiniolen	St Deiniolen	SH 54576593	950 f E Three old yews	Huge yews recorded in 1834. Neglected holy well nearby.
Llanelltyd	St Illtyd	SH 71751954	670 f S Two old yews	Medieval 'stone of Kenric' Circular yard.
Llangywer	SS Cywair & George	SH 90423226	730 f E	Redundant church near lake. Single immense yew.
Llanymawddwy	St Tydecho	SH 90331904	850+ ag f NE Five stems from old base	One ancient yew. Remote site on ancient route across mountains.
Maentwrog	St Twrog	SH 66454053	670 f SW Three old yews	Ancient 'Stone of Twrog' in the churchyard.
Mallwyd	St Tydecho	SH 86281235	1010 m E Three old yews	Historic church with unusual features. Yew with 19th C references.
Yspyty Ifan	St John	SH 84404890	485 f S Three female yews	Historic 'Pilgrim church' of St. John

North Wales and borderlands

Site	Dedication	Map Guide	Girth in centimetres	Site Notes
Cyffylliog	St Mary	SJ 05905783	890+ f E Three big yews.	Quiet valley site. Largest tree not on boundary.
Gresford (*Gresffordd*)	All Saints	SJ 34645497	885 m SE Many yews on site.	Iron railing around oldest much recorded yew. Early inscribed stone.
Gwyddelwern	St Beuno	SJ 07464668	470+ m E Fragment.	Enclosed in wall. Early Irish link.
Gwytherin **Detailed Study**	St Winifred	SH 87676147	880+ f E Two very old yews.	Historic site/ inscribed stone
Llanarmon D. Ceiriog	St Garmon	SJ 15833280	775 m W Two big yews.	Mound in churchyard. Yews either side of the path. Breton saint.
Llandderfel	St Derfel	SH 98163706	535+ m W Fragment	Historic churchyard. Derfel's wooden horse in porch. Lost yew.
Llandrillo	St Trillo	SJ 03433707	Un f S Two pieces.	Wall around amazing tree depicted in *Gentleman's Magazine* in the late 19th C. Well by river.
Llangadwaladr	St Cadwaladr	SJ 18163036	770+ f W Line of yews on old boundary.	Isolated single chambered church by stream.
Llangernyw **Detailed Study**	St Digain	SH 87526744	1020+ m N Many stems.	Inscribed stones on site.
Llangynog	St Cynog	SJ 05302610	Un f SW	Early medieval dedication. Single low branching tree.

Site	Dedication	Map Guide	Girth in centimetres	Site Notes
Llangwm	St Jerome	SH 96674460	915 f W Two parts.	Disused church. Giant old spreading yew. Rowan growing out of twisted limb.
Llansilin	St Silin	SJ 20962819	880+ m SE Six yews.	Five trees over 7m. Yews recorded by Borrow in 1854.
Llantysilio	St Tysilio	SJ 19404355	430 m W Fragment.	Redundant church site. Remains of tree still grows.
Nant Glyn	St James	SJ 00416213	730+ m S	Pulpit in heart of fine old yew.
Overton	St Mary	SH 37354181	475 m NW Fragment. Twenty two+ yews.	One of 'Seven wonders of Wales'. One very old yew. Modern iron rail.
Pennant Melangell **Detailed Study**	St Melangell	SJ 02422654	870 m E Five+ yews.	Historic early site.

Central Wales north

Site	Dedication	Map Guide	Girth in centimetres	Site Notes
Buttington	All Saints	SJ 24980884	820 m SW	Historic site. Skulls dug last century. Largest yew 1200 years old by tradition - west of church.
Carno	St John the Baptist	SN 96329648	700+ f W	Ass. Knights Hospitallers. Inscribed stone in church. Modern ass. Laura Ashley. Impressive yew.

Site	Dedication	Map Guide	Girth in centimetres	Site Notes
Guilsfield (*Cedigfa*)	St Aelhaiarn	SJ 21921165	360+ f 22 yews.	One yew with historical record approx. 380 yrs old. Interesting church.
Llanerfyl **Detailed Study**	St Erfyl	SJ 03400977	Un f S One male limb. Collapsed crown.	Inscribed stone & reliquary.
Llandinam	St Llonio	SO 02648860	760 f S Three main limbs	Tradition states 800yr old yew. Llonio a 6th C Saint. A *clas* site (mother church)
Llangynyw	St Cynyw	SJ 12710909	690 m W Four old yews.	Whitewashed church with oak porch.
Llanwnog	St Gwynnog	SO 02239382	700+ f E Nine yews.	Two largest yews either side of path by east gate.
Llanwrin	St Gwrin	SH 78660353	820+ m E Re-growth from cuts.	Dedication originally SS Ust & Dyfrig. West side of Dyfi valley.
Machynlleth	St Peter	SH 74530095	Un m E 3 main stems.	Dedication probably to St Cybi. Parish church in historic town at head of Dyfi estuary.
Manafon	St Michael	SJ 11300247	740 f SW Two yews.	Yews heavily pruned, biggest by gate. Poet R.S. Thomas once Rector.
Penegoes	St Cadfarch	SH 76840093	900+ m E	Well site across road. Old place name Llangadfarch

Central Wales south

Site	Dedication	Map Guide	Girth in centimetres	Site Notes
Aberedw	St Cewydd	SO 08024731	670 f NW Several Yews	Porch once used by musicians. 6th C St Cewydd has only two dedications.
Alltmawr	St Mauritius	SJ 07344687	870 m W	Unusual dedication. Very small church & yard with very big yew. Opp. side of Wye from Aberedw.
Casgob	St Michael & All Angels	S0 23906639	760 f W	D shaped enclosure with a stream on south side. On lower slopes of Radnor Forest.
Cefnllys	St Michael	SO 08476150	600 m E Several old yews.	Remote church by Afon Ithon. Castle mound & deserted village nearby.
Cregrina	St David	SO 12365210	800 m W Two old yews.	Church on old drovers' route above Afon Edw.
Disgoed	St Michael	SO 27666474	900+ m N Two old yews, the largest almost unm.	Holy well by gate. Largest yew split with much new growth.
Llanafan Fawr	St Afan	SN 96915578	970 f E Many-stemmmed yew.	Large circular churchyard. Inscribed stones.
Llanbadarn-y-Garreg	St Padarn	SO 11254877	450 m W Fragment.	Remote white-washed church next to river. Leaning yew has internal stem.
Llandeilo Graban	St Teilo	SO 09374468	790 m SW Three old yews.	The only Radnor dedication to Teilo. Hilltop site above Wye.

Site	Dedication	Map Guide	Girth in centimetres	Site Notes
Llanfaredd	St Mary	SO 06955075	910 f W	Small single chambered church. Huge female yew on western boundary
Llanfihangel Abergwesyn	St Michael	SN 85405268	790 m S Seven yews (six old)	Both sites without churches but yews remain. One tree, closest to road both m/f characteristics
Llanddewi Abergwesyn	St David	SN 85215272	610 f SW One yew with younger growth.	Opposite side of river.
Llanfihangel Nant Melan	St Michael	SO 18015818	800+ m SW Twin trunk. Five yews.	12th C. church ass. Knights Hospitallers. Yews grow on old boundary bank.
Llansantffraed-in-Elvel (*Llansantffraed-yn-Elfael*)	St Brigid	SO 09965486	770 m SW Many old yews.	Younger yews probably seedlings from original trees. Site of Cistercian nunnery in early 12th C.
Llanyre	St Llyr	SO 04456231	710 m N Four old yews.	Tradition states that Church was built on an ancient barrow.
Nantmel	St Cynllo	SO 03436637	850 f S Ring of old yews.	Other dedications to St Cynllo at Llangunllo and Llanbister.
Rhulen (*Rhiwlen*)	St David	SO 09374468 SO 13774984	800 f NE Yews on east and south boundary.	Unmodernised church, one of a small collection of David dedications in this area.
Whitton	St David	SO 27056733	700 m SW Several big yews.	Village church site near line of Offa's Dyke.

The Brecon region

Site	Dedication	Map Guide	Girth in centimetres	Site Notes
Aberllynfi (Three Cocks)		SO 17303801 Privately owned land.	560+ m Hollow yew. Much elder growth.	Medieval site. Church fell into disrepair in 18th C. Yew only remaining feature.
Aberysgir	SS Cynidr & Mary	SO 00042966	620 f S Two old yews.	Double dedicated church north of river Usk. Yews either side of path.
Betws Penpont	Unknown	SN 97252928	810 m NE Thirty+ yews.	Church with unusual round tower. One truly old yew of many in churchyard.
Capel-y-ffin	St Mary	SO 25493151	600 f SE Fragment. Five old yews.	Small whitewashed 'boundary chapel' rebuilt in 1762. Site of Benedictine Monastery nearby.
Defynnog **Detailed Study**	St Cynog	SN 92542793	1130 f N Four 'ancient' yews.	One of the most important yew tree sites in Wales. Inscribed stone. A *clas* site. Saint legends.
Llandefalle	St Matthew	SO 10733549	500+ f S Male similar in size. Other yews on site.	Large whitewashed church on hill. Stump of big yew east of church.
Llanelli	St Elli	SN 23231485	600+ f E Thirteen+ yews.	Almost complete circle of yews on an old embankment.
Llanfeugan	St Meugan	SO 08672453	920 f NE Twelve yews.	Meugan an early saint. Long narrow churchyard contains many yews. No village.

Site	Dedication	Map Guide	Girth in contimetres		Site Notes
Llanfoist	St Faith	SO 28631320	800	f S	Yew fire damaged 19th C. drawing by E. Lees.
Llansantffraed juxta Usk	St Brigid	SO 12242349	720	f W	Church near river Usk. Burial place of poet & scholar Henry Vaughan.
Llanspyddid (*Llansbyddyd*)	St Cattwg	SO 01192818	880 f NW Eight old yews.		Reputed burial place of Brychan's father Anlach. Early inscribed stone associated with him dated 7th/8th C.
Llanwenarth Citra	St Peter	SO 27551481	790 f SW Pronounced lean.		Large churchyard on floodplain of the Usk.
Mamheilad	St Illtyd	SO 30540344	950+ f S Five old yews.		Re-whitewashed church on hilltop site. Much recorded 'ancient' yew.
Merthyr Cynog	St Cynog	SN 98483745	760 m S Mature yews + younger growth.		Circular churchyard at centre of settle-ment. Reputed burial of Cynog.
Talgarth	St Gwendoline	SO 15733382	730 f S Split tree. Other yews on site.		Possible *clasau* site. Gwendoline reputedly buried at Talgarth. Biggest yew divides low and has wide spreading crown.
Ystradfellte	St Mary	SN 93061344	1040 m N Several old walled yews.		Historic valley site. Biggest yew wide spread limbs (cut off).

Wye Valley and Vale of Usk

Site	Dedication	Map Guide	Girth in centimetres	Site Notes
Betws Newydd	undedicated	SO 36220587	1000+ f W Several big yews.	Church with rood screen, loft and tympanum. Largest yew with internal stem depicted in 19th C. drawing
Goetre	St Peter	SO 32710592	670 f S Three big yews + stumps	One yew at churchyard boundary wall.
Llanarth	St Teilo	SO 37561096	990 f E	Historic church site with St Teilo's well outside churchyard.
Llanddewi Rhydderch	St David	SO 34991296	700 f E Yew grows close to church.	Yew has large internal stem.
Llanfair Discoed *(Llanfair Is-coed)*	St Mary	ST 44639242	680 f S	Neighbouring ruins of castle.
Llanfair Kilgeddin *(Llanfair Cilgedin)*	St Mary	SO 35590869	830 f S Two old yews.	Redundant church with rare paintings by river Usk. Some way from village centre.
Llanllowell *(Llanllywel)*	St Llywel	ST 39269858	720 m SE Split tree.	Split yew with branch brace. Small stream nearby.
Llansoy *(Llan-soe)*	St Tysoi	SO 44210239	870 m S	Big spreading yew.
Pen-allt	St Mary	SO 52191073	730 f E	'The old' church has square military style tower. Old sundial. Site high above river Wye.
Tredunnock *(Tredynog)*	St Andrew	ST 37999485	500+ f S	Inscribed stone in church at centre of village.

South Wales

Site	Dedication	Map Guide	Girth in centimetres	Site Notes
Glyncorrwg	St John the Baptist	SS 87429930	660 f S Twin stemmed. Four yews.	Reference in 1810 to 'five remarkable yews'. Three remain.
Ilston (*Llanilltyd Gŵyr*)	St Illtyd	SS 55669034	518 f S	Big tall spreading yew growing on mound. River Ilston flows by churchyard.
Llanedern	St Edern	ST 22058199	820 m S Fragment	Whitewashed church. Sloping site. Tree with much recent fire damage.
Llanmihangel (*Llanfihangel y Bont-faen*)	St Michael	SS 98137189	635 m S	St Anne's well outside churchyard. 16th C. house across road.
Llanrhidian	SS Illtyd & Rhidian	SS 49629223	620 f S + stump	Fort like tower. 'Leper stone' in porch. Overlooks salt marsh.
Mynyddislwyn	St Tudor	ST 19349391	700 m N Six old yews. (five in a line).	Hilltop site. Unusual church tower. St Tudor's mound adjacent to churchyard.
Pendoylan (*Pendeulwyn*)	St Cadoc	ST 05977668	790 m E Two stems.	Growing on mound. A futher old yew on boundary slope.
St Brides-super-Ely (*Llansanffraed-ar-Eléai*)	St Bride	ST 09687762	745 m SE	Anglicised St Brigid. Small church.
Ystradgynlais	St Cynog	SN 78701007	700+ f N	Early saints dedication. Yew grows within an uncemented wall.

West Wales

Site	Dedication	Map Guide	Girth in centimetres	Site Notes
Cenarth	St Llawddog	SN 27034150	Un m E Fragment.	Walled yew. Limb recently fell in storm. Inscribed stone. Close to river Teifi.
Cilycwm	St Michael	SN 75334002	730 m SE Five yews.	Unusual looking male tree. River flows behind church.
Llandybie	St Tybie	SN 61831555	640 m S	Church with some unusual features. Much pruned yew beside entrance gate.
Llanfihangel Abercywyn	St Michael	SN 30201330 Access across private farm land.	500+ f S	Isolated ruin of 'pilgrim' church overlooking Taff estuary.
Llangathen	St Cathen	SN 58442214	590 m S Several big yews.	Fortified church tower. Hilltop site near Aberglasney Gardens.
Llanfair Clydogau	St Mary	SN 62445124	730 f E	Near river and bridge. Big yew grows within wall.
Llanfihangel Genau'r Glyn	St Michael	SN 62328690	1060+ f N A fragment with three remaining stems	Restored holy well. Area of much scenic and natural history interest. Graves in woodland.
Llanfihangel Ystrad	St Michael	SN 52455622	850+ f S	Church in village by river Aeron. Huge old free that has regrown after pruning.
Llangeitho	St Ceitho	SN 62056009	590 m W Several old yews.	Churchyard on edge of village. Yews recorded in 1890's.

Site	Dedication	Map Guide	Girth in centimetres	Site Notes
Llangybi	St Cybi	SO 60865318	Un f S Leaning tree.	Famous restored holy well 400 m away. Churchyard by bridge on old road.
Nevern (*Nyfer*)	St Brynach	SN 08334002	Avenue of eight yews leading from gate to porch.	'Bleeding yew of Nevern'. Large Celtic cross and early Christian inscribed stones.
St Dogmaels (*Llandudoch*)	St Mary's Abbey	SN 16354585	Un f S Frag.	Early inscribed memorial stone in church beside Abbey ruins. Yew grows in high wall by porch.
Ystrad-ffin	St Paulinus	SN 78764704	740+ m SW	Remote chapel site in mountain area beside RSPB Dinas Reserve.
Strata Florida (*Ystrad Fflur*)	St Mary	SN 74606580	670 f N Many old yews.	Historic abbey site of much interest. Old churchyard has two ancient yews. Pre-Norman marked stone. Burial place of Dafydd ap Gwilym, famous Welsh poet.

Main sources used

Arnold, C. J. & Davies, J.L.: *Roman & Early Medieval Wales* (Stroud, 2000)

Baxter, T.: *The Eternal Yew* (Hanley Swan, 1992)

Bevan-Jones, R.: *The Ancient Yew, a History of Taxus baccata,* (Macclesfield, 2002)

Borrow, G.: *Wild Wales,* London, 1862, (ed. Collins, 1955)

Brash, R. R.: *Archaeologia Cambrensis,* vol. 1870

Breverton, T. D.: *The Book of Welsh Saints* (Cowbridge, 2000)

Brueton, D. & Chetan, A.: *The Sacred Yew* (London, 1994)

Bryce, D. (ed.): S. Baring Gould & J. Fisher, *Lives of the British Saints*   (Llanerch, 2006)

Carey, J.: *King of Mysteries, Early Irish Religious Writings*(Dublin, 1998)

Caseldine, A. E.: *Montgomeryshire Collections 82* (Dept. of Arch., UWL, 1994)

Cornish, V.: *The Churchyard Yew and Immortality* (London, 1946)

Davies, J. R.: *The Book of Llandaff and the Norman Church in Wales* (Woodbridge, 2003)

Davis, P.: *Sacred Springs* (Abergavenny, 2003)

Doble, G. H.: *Lives of the Welsh Saints* (3rd ed., Cardiff, 1993)

Edwards, N. & Lane, A.: *The Early Church in Wales and the West* (Oxford, 1992)

Evans J. D.: *The Churchyard Yews of Gwent* (Pontypool, 1988)

Gregory, D.: *Country Churchyards in Wales* (Llanwrst, 1991)

Hartzell, H.: *The Yew Tree, a Thousand Whispers* (Oregon, 1991)

James, H,: 'Early Medieval Cemeteries in Wales' in (eds) N. Edwards and A. Lane *The Early Church in Wales and the West* (Oxford,1992)

Jenkins, D. (trans. & ed.): *The Law of Hywel Da, Law Texts from Medieval Wales* (Llandysul, 1986)

Johns, C. A.: *British Trees and Shrubs* (London, 1860)

Jones, F.: *The Holy Wells of Wales* (3rd ed., Cardiff, 1998)

Knight, J.: 'Basilicas and Barrows: Christian Origins in Wales and Western Britain', in M. Carver (ed.), *The Cross goes North: Processions of Conversion in Northern Europe, 300-1300* (York, 2003)

Laing, L. & J.: *The Origins of Britain* (London, 1982)

Lees, E.: 'Old and Remarkable Yews' in *The Gardeners Chronicle,* 30th May 1874

Lewis, S.: *Topographical Dictionary of Wales,* (2nd ed., London, 1840)

Lhuyd, E.: 'Parochalia 1697', reprinted in *Archaeologia Cambrensis* (London, 1909-11)

Linnard, W.: *Welsh Woods and Forests: a history* (Llandysul, 2000)

Low, M.: *Celtic Christianity and Nature* (Edinburgh, 1996)

Lowe, J.: *The Yew Trees of Great Britain and Ireland* (London, 1897)

Lucas, A. T.: 'The Sacred Trees of Ireland', in *Journal of the Cork Historical and Archeological Society 68* (Cork, 1963)

Mac Cana, P.: *Celtic Mythology* (London, 1983)

Matthews, C. & J.: *The Encyclopaedia of Celtic Wisdom* (Dorset, 1994)

Nash-Williams, V.E.: *The Early Christian Monuments of Wales* (Cardiff, 1950)

Ó Corráin, D, Breatnach, P. & McCone, K (eds.): *Sages, Saints and Storytellers* (Maynooth, 1989)Owen, G. R.: *Rites and Religions of the Anglo Saxons* (London, 1996)

Pennant, T.: *Tours in Wales, 1784* (Caernarfon, 1883)

Price, T. S.: quoted in *Historic Landscape Characterisation* (CPAT)

Pryor, F.: *Britain BC* (London, 2004)

Radford, C. & Hemp, D (eds.): *Historia divae Monacellae, The History and the Cult of Saint Melangell* (1959)

Rees, E.: *Celtic Saints, Passionate Wanderers* (London, 2000)

Rees, W. J.: (trans.) *Liber Landavensis – The Ancient Register of the Cathedral Church of Llandaff (Llyfr Teilo)* (London, 1840)

Thacker, A. & Sharpe, R. (eds.): *Local Saints and Local Churches in the Medieval West* (Oxford, 2002)

Thomas, C.: *Christian Celts, Messages and Images* (Stroud, 1998)

Vaughan Thomas, W. & Llewellyn, A.: *The Shell Guide to Wales* (London, 1969)

Warner, R.,: *A Second Walk Through Wales* (1798)

Wheeler, R. T.: 'A Survey of Churchyard Yews' in *Clwyd Historian* (1984)

Wilkes, J. H.,: *Trees of the British Isles in History & Legend* (London, 1972)

Zaluckyj, S. & J: *The Celtic Christian Sites of the central and southern Marches* (Logaston, 2006)

Further reading

Alchin, A. M.: *Pennant Melangell: Place of Pilgrimage* (1994)

Ancient Yew Group: (regularly updated website)

Andrew, J.: 'Churchyard Yew Trees in the Archdeaconry of Gower' in *Gower* (1992)

Britnell, W. J.: 'Excavation and Recording at Pennant Melangell Church', in *Montgomeryshire Collections*, no. 82 (Welshpool, 1994)

Bowen, E. G.: *The Settlements of the Celtic Saints of Wales* (Cardiff, 1954)

Condry, W.: *Exploring Wales* (London, 1970)

Davies, W.: *Wales in the Early Middle Ages* (Leicester, 1982)

Dimock, J. E. (ed.): T. Forester & T. Wright, *Giraldi Cambrensis Opera* (London, 1867)

Graves, R.: *The White Goddess, A historical Grammar of poetic myth* (London, 1948)

Gray Hulse, T.: *Gwytherin: A Welsh Cult Site of the Mid Twelfth Century*, unpublished paper (April, 1994)

Hageneder, F.: *Yew: A History* (Stroud, 2007)

Hansard, G. A:. *The Book of Archery* (London, 1840)

Hardy, R: *The Longbow, A Social and Military History* (London, 1992)

Hinson, C. (trans.& ed.): *The National Gazetteer of Great Britain and Ireland* (London, 1868)

Hughes, T. J.: *Wales's Best One Hundred Churches* (Bridgend, 2006)

Hyde, H. A.: *Welsh Timber Trees*, National Museum of Wales (Cardiff, 1931)

Kelly, F.: *Early Irish Farming* (Dublin, 1997)

Laing, L.: *Celtic Britain* (London, 1981)

Lingard, W.: *Welsh Woods and Forests, A History* (Llandysul, 2007)

Mitchell, A.: *The Trees of Britain* (London, 1996)

Rackham, O.: *Trees and Woodland in the British Landscape* (London, 1976) *The History of the Countryside* (London, 1994)

Rhys, J.: *The Pagan Folklore of Welsh Wells* (Oxford, 1901)

Swanton, E. W.: *The Yew Trees of England* (Farnham, 1958)

Toulmin-Smith, L. (ed.): *The Itinerary of John Leland, in 1536-1539*, part 4, vol. 3 (London, 1964)